the cook &
the baker

To Naomi
Happy Baking

Best,

[signature]

The cook & the baker aims to inspire enjoyment in its readers, and for Global Baker Dean Brettschneider this is about placing baking firmly at the centre of events. Bakehouse shares Dean's passion for baking, and we are delighted to be working with him to complement our new product development plans.

Our wide range includes melt-in-the-mouth Danish pastries, buttery viennoiserie, tempting Continental savouries and versatile speciality breads. Each product is individually selected from our network of 15 European partner bakeries, all specialists in their field, enabling us to bring only the very best to our customers in the UK, Ireland, Australia and South Africa. Through this unique approach, Bakehouse offers levels of quality, authenticity and innovation that are second to none.

From our acclaimed All-Butter Croissant and our best-selling Cheese Twist, to our legendary Maple Pecan Plait and groundbreaking Rusticata breads, we have products for every part of the day.

BAKEHOUSE

www.bakehouse.co.uk

the cook &
the baker

SENSATIONAL RECIPES FROM
MARK MCDONOUGH &
DEAN BRETTSCHNEIDER

RANDOM HOUSE
NEW ZEALAND

GLOBAL BAKER Dean Brettschneider

A RANDOM HOUSE BOOK published by Random House New Zealand
18 Poland Road, Glenfield, Auckland, New Zealand

For more information about our titles go to www.randomhouse.co.nz

A catalogue record for this book is available from the National Library of New Zealand

Random House New Zealand is part of the Random House Group
New York London Sydney Auckland Delhi Johannesburg

First published 2010

© 2010 text Dean Brettschneider and Mark McDonough
© 2010 photography Aaron McLean

ISBN 978 1 86979 381 4

Design: Pieta Brenton
Photography: Aaron McLean
Styling: Donna North

Printed in China by 1010 Printing International Limited

contents

a word from the cook   6

a word from the baker   8

about the recipes in this book   9

breads   10

entrées   58

main meals   102

desserts   152

cakes, cookies, pastries & petits fours   172

basics   210

   basic baking techniques   212

   ingredients   228

   basic savoury recipes   235

   basic sweet recipes   242

weights & measures   246

acknowledgements   249

index   252

a word from the cook

I have a passion and that passion is for food. I love creating dishes that are tasty, flavoursome and relatively easy to prepare. Feeding a young family — that is my challenge. I don't get to cook commercially at Zarbo anymore as I am too busy being the face of the company, but I still love to cook at home. Most nights I cook dinner for my family. Simple foods, with a fresh flavour and quality ingredients — to me these are the key to successful home cooking.

Zarbo has been an exciting journey over the past 15 years, a journey that has been full of challenges but also full of rewards. I believe the key to the success of the business has been constant innovation and evolution, not only of the store but also of the food we sell, the products we stock and the training and attitude of our staff. I have always encouraged staff to engage and interact with our customers — it's great to see them talking to our customers and, in turn, to see these people becoming regulars at Zarbo.

Over the years, an amazing Zarbo community has developed — not only of staff and ex-staff but of loyal customers. There are so many customers I have gotten to know over the years who have become good friends to me and to my family. There are even customers whose children and grandchildren live overseas and who look to my kids as their surrogate grandchildren.

When travelling, I'm not only sourcing new products for the shelves but I'm also looking for new ideas about how to approach food and ingredients. I find inspiration to translate the dishes I enjoy into something that will work here in New Zealand. I also have an interest in dietary issues and restrictions that customers may have — I am helped with this by my wife, who is a doctor, but she also has a degree in nutrition. It's great to be able to ask questions and bounce ideas around with Cushla.

This collaboration follows the success of my three previous books and two diaries. I have been blown away by the success of these books and how well read and well used the recipes are. Constantly, I am being told by customers about the dishes they have made and about dishes that have become their firm favourites. It also amazes me how many of the books have been sent overseas as presents for friends and family. I am regularly told stories of how the books and recipes are being used in other parts of the world. I remember being in Richmond, London, a couple of years ago and being told of a café there that was making dishes out of my books. And, when a regular customer was travelling to Argentina and wanted to take a Kiwi gift for their host, I was asked to autograph a book for them to take. They arrived to find that the first meal their host had cooked for them was out of another Zarbo cookbook!

As with my previous books, the recipes here are dishes that are not too difficult for the home cook to replicate — they are dishes which have punch, maximum flavour and eye-appeal without the need for too much blood, sweat and tears. When I am developing recipes

I make sure that around 95 per cent of the ingredients are available in my supermarket or local Asian food store. That ensures that you, the reader, won't be dependent upon speciality food stores to source ingredients.

I believe that the food we cook should be in tune with the seasons and I also believe that it is important to develop great relationships with local suppliers. The independent fishmonger, butcher and greengrocer are fast becoming a thing of the past so, please, support these people. By doing so, when you need that particular vegetable or cut of meat for a special dish you wish to try out they will go out of their way to help you.

All over the country we are seeing the emergence of Farmers' Markets — these are a great place to source ingredients. The producers and growers that you meet at the markets can be real characters and it's great to see their passion for the products that they grow and/or process. I have also included in this book a few fruits that are not grown in New Zealand but are now readily available in the market at certain times of the year, such as pomegranate, pawpaw and mango. You can buy these ripe and ready to use immediately or buy them unripened — stored correctly you can extend their season.

Dean and I have known each other for many years. I'm not quite sure how we first met, but it was in the Auckland foodie community. From our first meetings I recall his passion for baking and his drive to become the best. I have watched his career develop over the years from that of a Kiwi with a can-do attitude to someone who is truly a Global Baker.

One of the first things Dean did when he came back to New Zealand was to come to Zarbo for breakfast. It was on these visits that the idea of the Global Baker Zarbo micro bakery was hatched. It was a logical extension of my brand to include a bakery in the business. I could have scoured the world looking for the right concept and person to consult, but who could be better than Dean? Over time the concept evolved and, after much discussion about designs, layout and where in-store it should be located, the concept was developed. After a couple of trips up to Shanghai to look at Dean's micro-bakery Slice I was convinced that it would work here and in July 2009 the Global Baker Zarbo micro bakery opened.

Even before the bakery opened Dean and I had discussed doing a book together, combining our individual strengths to create a unique book. Dean and I share a vision and a passion not only for the food we create, not only for New Zealand's place in the culinary world, but also for business. We both have a fascination and, I believe, a great understanding of how to offer our customers great products and services in a way that sets us apart. Our approach to this book will hopefully inspire you to want to try out these recipes at home. Good luck!

Mark McDonough

a word from the baker

New Zealand is a nation of hunters and gathers and because we are a young country many of us travel to explore other cultures. In typical Kiwi fashion we gather ideas as we go and set-to to develop new products that suit many different cultures' needs. I have travelled widely and sharing knowledge has always been a focus for me, which is one of the reasons why I decided to write my first book on New Zealand baking in 1999. This is my sixth book

When I began thinking about this book the first question I asked myself was: How can I place baking at the centre of the dining table? The time has come for bakers across the globe to take their work to a new level to match the work of chefs and cooks. After all, a complete dining experience cannot happen without the work of the humble baker — from the breads served at the start of a meal, to the dessert and, finally, the petits fours sometimes served as an encore to a grand dining experience. When using these recipes, I hope you will take the time to honour the art of baking.

I first met Mark in Auckland in early 2000 and became a frequent customer of Zarbo. I thoroughly enjoyed everything that Zarbo stood for as a food destination, but there was an obvious omission. In 2005 I mentioned to Mark that what he needed was a micro bakery within Zarbo — it would be a New Zealand first for the café and deli scene.

On my regular visits to New Zealand it became a ritual that Susan, Jason and I would stop for breakfast at Zarbo after our early morning arrival from Shanghai. Each time, Mark and I would become engaged in developing the micro-bakery concept. You could almost say the beginnings of the bakery were like making a good loaf of bread — deciding what to make, selecting the right, quality ingredients, mixing the dough, setting it aside to ferment, shaping it, and giving it its final rising before decorating and baking. This organic process was almost exactly how we went about bringing Global Baker Zarbo micro bakery to life!

Mark and I share the same passion, vision and, most of all, a respect for each other's professionalism in creating exceptional food for others to enjoy. Summed up, you could say, 'Do it right or you don't do it at all' and 'Often, less is more'. Zarbo's simple philosophy is the same as the one we adopt at Baker & Spice in Shanghai. Both businesses have a Euro-Antipodean focus and, always, there is a drive for excellence.

When I think of key words to represent the food we make I think 'fresh, simple, clean, wholesome, natural, honest, rustic and flavoursome. All these words represent home-style baking, but there's a lot of experience, knowledge, technical understanding and passion thrown into the mix to take the baking from ordinary to extra-ordinary. That's my style. For me, baking is a 24-hour-a-day, seven-day-a-week, 365-day-a-year job. Happy Baking!

Dean Brettschneider

about the recipes in this book

This book is not just another recipe book. It's a collection of baking and cooking related influences from throughout Dean Brettschneider's and Mark McDonough's lives. However, there are many recipes — some classic and some that have been turned on their heads regarding flavour combinations, texture, style and cultural eating habits.

Some people will gain inspiration from looking at the wonderful photographs while others will be attracted by the interesting recipes. But the most important thing for us is that you enjoy getting your hands into the doughs and batters, chopping and peeling those vegetables to prepare the perfect stock, and shopping to buy the best cut of beef and freshest fillet of fish required to make these recipes come to life.

Please read through each recipe, twice even, before you embark on making them, as some require advance preparation. Over and above all of the recipes and information in this book, one of the most important aspects of preparing a dinner party is to have fun. We hope you will enjoy this experience and, most of all, this book.

breads

breads

A good bread is one of the most simple pleasures in life when served
with a nice piece of cheese and a good bottle of wine. When you embark
on making a loaf of bread, you are setting out on a journey — you know
where you have to start and you know where you want to end up, but the
experiences you have along the way will vary. They can be exhilarating
and enjoyable when everything goes well and challenging when things
don't go according to plan. All the planning, buying ingredients, measuring
ingredients, mixing dough, resting dough in the right conditions, shaping
it, allowing it to rise again, placing it in the oven at exactly the right time
and temperature and, finally, taking it out of the oven at the exact moment
when it's baked and hearing it sing when the crust is cracking as it cools —
as far as I'm concerned anticipating and opening Christmas presents isn't
as exciting as that.

All this magic is brought about with flour, water, salt, yeast, passion,
dedication, commitment and fun — the essential ingredients for a perfect
loaf of bread. People laugh at me when I say that if you're happy the bread
you make will be exceptional. Equally, if you're in a bad mood the bread
will be substandard. It amazes me that many people think of bread as a
commodity — it is far from that as it features in daily life around the globe.

Bread is not just about yeast, so I have included quick-breads made with
baking powder and or soda, breads enriched with butter, sugar, and eggs,
and bread-related dishes. Finally, by adding passion and practice to the
bread-making process, I know you will exceed your own expectations and
realise that making bread is one of the most satisfying things to do in the
kitchen.

the baker

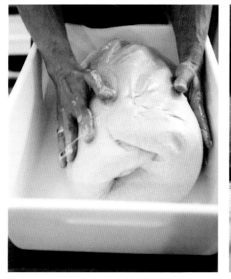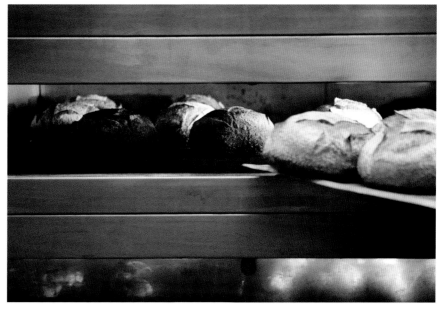

mini wholewheat irish soda bread sandwiches with smoked salmon, onion marmalade & dill mayonnaise

makes 2 small loaves and serves 4

Soda bread is a thing of the past, but the inclusion of the seeds and grains make this moist and healthy and the touch of honey adds a little sweetness. Enjoy with any meal or made into sandwiches as served here.

dough

115g plain flour
5g baking powder
$\frac{1}{2}$ teaspoon baking soda
$\frac{1}{2}$ teaspoon cream of tartar
good pinch of salt
115g wholewheat or wholemeal flour
20g sunflower seeds
20g linseeds

20g sesame seeds
25g pumpkin seeds
20g rolled oats
10g honey
200ml milk
115g natural yoghurt

rolled oats for decoration

Sift the plain flour, baking powder, baking soda, cream of tartar and salt into a large mixing bowl. Add the wholewheat or wholemeal flour, all the seeds and the rolled oats and stir together. Add the honey, milk and natural yoghurt. Using a wooden spoon, stir the mixture together until well combined and a batter-like consistency — you are not looking for an elastic dough so don't be alarmed or tempted to add more flour.

Spoon the mixture into greased mini loaf tins and level the tops smooth, then sprinkle with rolled oats. Using a small knife dipped in oil, cut into the dough lengthways, halfway down into the batter to create a place for the loaf to split when rising during the first stages of baking.

Bake for 35–40 minutes in a preheated oven set at 180–190°C until a cake skewer comes out clean when inserted. Remove from the oven and tip loaves onto a cooling rack.

sandwich filling

50g onion jam per sandwich
  (see page 239)
200g smoked salmon slices

small bunch of dill, finely chopped and
  mixed in with the lemon juice and
  mayonnaise

1 tsp mayonnaise per sandwich   salt and pepper to taste
1 tsp lemon juice per sandwich

To serve, cut the cooled bread into 8 slices (for top and bottom of each sandwich) and spread a small amount of onion jam on 4 of the slices. Top with slices of smoked salmon and a dollop of dill mayonnaise. Season to taste. Serve as individual sandwiches, each on its own serving plate.

sunflower & paprika rolls served with antipasti

makes 30 rolls

These little rolls are frequently on the bread menu at The Providores Restaurant in London, owned by Peter Gordon — a fellow Kiwi and a good friend of mine. Where possible, use sweet smoked paprika. You will notice the difference.

dough

500g strong bread flour

10g salt

10g sugar

5g instant dried yeast

10g olive oil

10g paprika powder, the sweet smoked type if possible

340ml water (more or less)

160g sunflower seeds

additional flour for dusting

4–5 ice cubes for creating steam in the oven

Using a wooden spoon, mix all the ingredients together in a large mixing bowl (except the sunflower seeds) until a dough mass has formed. Tip the dough out onto a lightly floured surface and knead for 10–15 minutes until the dough is smooth and elastic in feel. Take a rest period of 30 seconds every 2–3 minutes. Add the sunflower seeds and knead through until evenly distributed. Lightly oil a bowl large enough to allow the dough to double in bulk, then put the dough into the bowl and cover with lightly oiled plastic wrap. Leave in a warmish place (23–25°C) for 1 hour. Knock back the dough in the bowl by gently folding it back onto itself. This will deflate it slightly, but allow it to develop more strength. Cover again with plastic wrap and set aside for 30 minutes. Knock back the dough once more and re-cover with plastic wrap. Place dough in the refrigerator overnight.

The next day, gently tip the dough onto a lightly floured bench and divide into 20 equal pieces — approximately 40g each. Roll each dough piece into a small ball or mini-baguette shape and place rolls on 2 baking trays lined with non-stick baking paper. Cover each tray with a sheet of plastic wrap and allow to rise for 1–1½ hours, depending on the room temperature — the dough should be slightly springy to the touch, almost a little under-proofed.

If you like you can dust the rolls with flour, then using a sharp pointed pair of scissors or sharp knife snip 3 cuts into each roll or 2 cuts into each mini baguette.

Place in a preheated oven set at 220–230°C with a small ovenproof dish in the bottom shelf. Quickly throw the ice cubes into the heated ovenproof dish to create steam. Bake for 15–18 minutes. Remove from the oven and transfer onto a cooling rack.

(Continued overleaf.)

To serve warm for dinner, place rolls on a baking tray and heat in a preheated oven set at 200°C for 5–8 minutes until nice and crisp.

antipasti
100g black kalamata olives
4 good-sized artichokes hearts, cooked and marinated in olive oil and herbs
onion jam (see page 239)
100g sun-dried tomatoes
100g stuffed bell peppers
100g grilled eggplant
100g grilled capsicum
micro salad leaves dressed with olive oil

To serve, place the rolls onto a serving plate and serve with a selection of chilled antipasti.

bruschetta plate

serves 4

When it's time for sharing, this tapas plate is great, especially when you serve your guests their own individual plates. The options for toppings are endless and you can make up your own depending on what is in season. Allow 3 slices per person — one of each topping combo.

1 baguette or ciabatta loaf
extra virgin olive oil

Cut the baguette or ciabatta into slices 1cm thick. Brush with olive oil and bake in a preheated oven set at 150°C until a light golden brown and crisp.

blue cheese & fig jam topping

200g dried figs
1 teaspoon fresh lemon juice
1 cup water

2 tablespoons maple syrup
pinch of salt
75g blue cheese

Remove the stems from the figs and place in a food processor with the lemon juice and process until roughly chopped. Put the chopped figs, water, maple syrup and salt in a saucepan, bring to the boil, lower the heat and simmer for approximately 25 minutes until thick. Transfer to a bowl, cover and cool.

Spread fig jam on the toasted bread, then crumble blue cheese on top.

tomato & basil topping

2–3 vine-ripened tomatoes
small bunch of basil leaves

extra virgin olive oil
salt and pepper to taste

Cut the tomatoes in half and remove the seeds, then cut into small cubes. Cut the basil into small pieces and toss together with the tomatoes and olive oil. Season with salt and pepper.

Place mixed tomato and basil on the toasted bread.

salami & rocket with lemon dressing topping & goat's cheese topping

1 cup fresh rocket
lemon dressing (see page 237)

salami
50g crumbly goat's cheese

Lightly dress the rocket with lemon dressing. Place 2 slices of salami on each bruschetta and then top with lemony rocket and sprinkle with goat's cheese.

To serve, place 1 of each bruschetta on a plate per person and serve immediately.

whipped brie de meaux & crouton mille-feuille with rocket salad

serves 4

Whipping cheese might sound a little strange, but it works well with soft cheeses such as brie and camembert or even a creamy blue cheese. This is really a cheese plate with crisp breads and demonstrates how cheese can be great served at the start of dinner rather than at the end. The balsamic glaze brings a nice acidic sweetness to the cheese. Ensure you take a forkful of all the textures to really enjoy the contrast.

12 thin baguette slices
extra virgin olive oil
sea salt
350g ripe brie, rind removed, chilled
balsamic reduction (see page 242)
freshly ground pepper
1 cup fresh rocket
sea salt

Brush both sides of each slice of baguette with the extra virgin olive oil and sprinkle with a little sea salt. Bake in a preheated oven set at 150°C for 10–15 minutes until golden brown and crisp. Cool and store in an airtight container until required — it's best to make the croutons a few hours before you need them.

Place the chilled brie in the small bowl of an electric mixer fitted with a beater attachment and beat on medium speed for approximately 10 minutes until it is very white and creamy — you will need to scrape down the sides of the bowl 2–3 times.

Using the balsamic reduction in a squirty bottle, make a series of random circles on 4 serving plates. Using a tablespoon dipped in hot water make a quenelle — a small oval scoop — with the whipped brie. Place the quenelle of brie in the centre of the plate, then sprinkle with pepper and place a crouton at an angle on top. Make another quenelle, and place it angled on top, sprinkle with pepper and then place the second crouton on top. You should have 2 quenelles separated by 2 croutons. Repeat the process to make 3 more servings.

Toss the rocket in a little extra virgin olive oil and place a small pile on top of each mille-feuille. Sprinkle with sea salt and serve.

bagel crisps & grissini

serves 4

Bagels are from New York and grissini are from Italy — together they make a perfect match for a selection of dips with different and interesting flavours and textures. I like to serve them with eggplant dip, brandade dip and olive tapenade (see pages 236–238).

bagel crisps

4 plain, day-old bagels   extra virgin olive oil

Using a very sharp serrated bread knife, cut each bagel horizontally into circles 3mm thick. Brush each circle on both sides with olive oil and bake in a preheated oven set at 150°C for 15–20 minutes until lightly toasted and dried out. Store in an airtight container until required.

grissini bread sticks

300g bread flour

5g salt

5g sugar

10g fresh yeast or 1 teaspoon
   of instant dried yeast

20g olive oil

$1/_2$ teaspoon of aniseed, lightly bruised
   in a mortar and pestle

180ml water

black and white sesame seeds for
   decoration (optional)

Using a wooden spoon, mix all the ingredients except the sesame seeds in a large mixing bowl to form a sticky dough. Tip the dough out onto a lightly floured surface and knead for 10–15 minutes until the dough is smooth and elastic in feel. Take a rest period of 30 seconds every 2–3 minutes. Don't be tempted to add excessive amounts of flour during the kneading process — but a little will be okay.

Lightly oil a bowl large enough to allow the dough to double in bulk, then put the dough into the bowl and cover with lightly oiled plastic wrap. Leave in a warmish place (23–25°C) for 1 hour. Knock back the dough in the bowl by gently folding it back onto itself. This will deflate it slightly, but allow it to develop more strength. Cover again with plastic wrap and leave for 30 minutes.

Tip the dough onto a lightly floured bench, then flatten it into a rectangular shape about 5mm thick. Cover for 10 minutes. Using a large sharp knife cut dough into 3 strips about 5mm across and 30cm long. Roll each strip into a long stick shape, lightly brush with water and dip into the sesame seeds, if using, and place on a baking tray lined with non-stick baking paper. Make sure the sticks aren't too thick — they should be around 5mm in diameter. Cover with plastic wrap and leave for 15–20 minutes to rise a little.

Bake for 20–25 minutes in a preheated oven set at 220°C until dried out. Remove from the oven and transfer to a cooling rack. Store in an airtight container until required.

poilâne miche-style
pain au levain

makes 1 very large loaf

I have always been impressed by the work of the Poilâne family, especially the strong baking traditions of the late Lionel Poilâne that are now practised by his daughter Apollonia. But because I don't believe in copying other people's products, I have developed a similar loaf that reflects my own baking values. Out of respect for the Poilâne tradition, I have called this loaf Poilâne Miche-style pain au levain and, like its inspiration, it's a larger-than-life loaf — 2kg dough weight. It can be kept for a week and used by cutting the loaf in half, then into quarters, as required.

600g strong bread flour
200g wholemeal flour
200g rye flour
350g levain (see page 221)
20g malt flour (enzyme-active
   malt flour is best)

25g salt
700ml chilled water (more or less)

additional flour for dusting
4–5 ice cubes for creating steam
   in the oven

Using a wooden spoon, mix all the ingredients together in a large mixing bowl to form a dough mass. Tip the dough onto a lightly floured surface and knead for 12–15 minutes until it is smooth and elastic in feel. Take a rest period of 30 seconds every 2–3 minutes. Place the dough into a lightly oiled bowl large enough for the dough to double in size and cover with lightly oiled plastic wrap. Leave in a warm place for up to 3 hours until almost doubled in size. Tip the dough onto the bench and gently knock back by folding it onto itself 3–4 times. Return the dough to the lightly oiled bowl and cover with the plastic wrap and set aside in a warm place for another hour. The dough should be really gassy and bubbly by now — full of life and energy!

Gently tip the dough onto a lightly floured bench and very gently mould it into a large round ball. Cover and set aside to rest for 15–20 minutes. While the dough is resting, lay a tea towel inside a very large round cane basket or round bowl large enough for the dough to double in size and heavily dust it with flour to create an even layer on which the dough will rest while rising for its final time. Alternatively, use a linen-lined proving basket brackets (called a benneton in French).

Mould the dough into its final ball shape, making sure the ball is tight and firm and the seam is at the bottom. Gently place the dough into the prepared basket or bowl with the smooth side down and the scrunched seam side up. Cover with plastic wrap or put inside a plastic supermarket shopping bag. Set aside in a warm place for 1 hour. Transfer to the refrigerator overnight — maximum 12 hours — to develop the flavour

(Continued overleaf.)

and texture of the cooked loaf.

Remove the dough from the refrigerator and leave to rise at room temperature for 4–5 hours. The final proving time will depend on the room temperature. Press the dough with your finger — if it leaves an indentation, it is fully proved.

Gently tip loaf seam side down onto a baking stone or baking tray preheated to 250°C. Using a sharp knife or razor blade, make 4 cuts or 2 half circles into the top surface of the dough. Put the loaf on the lower-middle shelf of the preheated oven set at 250°C with a small ovenproof dish in the bottom shelf. Quickly throw the ice cubes into the heated ovenproof dish to create steam. Bake for 30 minutes and then turn the loaf around, reduce the oven temperature to 200°C and bake for a further 40–45 minutes until the crust is a dark golden brown colour and when the bottom is tapped the loaf sounds hollow. Remove from the oven and transfer the loaf to a cooling rack.

fresh chunky apple, roasted hazelnut, thyme & cabernet sauvignon rustico bread

makes 2 or 3 rectangular loaves

This idea came from two loaves of bread I found in Tokyo — one was made with apple cider and the other with red wine. I simply combined the two, but felt that a little nuttiness was needed so I roasted some hazelnuts and threw them into the mix. Be warned, this is a two-day process — you will need to make the biga ferment the day before you make the bread.

biga ferment

225g strong bread flour

20g wholemeal flour

1g instant dried yeast

135ml Cabernet Sauvignon, chilled

Mix all the ingredients together in a bowl to form a firm, elastic dough. Place into an oiled container, cover and ferment for 18–24 hours (overnight) at room temperature.

dough

100g Granny Smith apples, peeled and cut into ¹/₂ cm cubes

juice of 1 lemon

75g hazelnuts

1 quantity biga ferment (see above)

245g strong bread flour

2g instant dried yeast

1 tablespoon fresh thyme, chopped

10g salt

250ml Cabernet Sauvignon, chilled

additional flour for dusting

4–5 ice cubes for creating steam in the oven

Cover the cubed apple with lemon juice to avoid browning and set aside until required. Roast the hazelnuts at 180°C until amber in colour, then roughly chop. Place remaining ingredients in the bowl of an electric mixer fitted with a beater. Mix on low speed until a rough dough is formed. Continue to mix on medium speed for 5–6 minutes until the dough is smooth, silky and almost fully developed. You may need to scrape down the sides of the bowl from time to time to ensure all the dough is getting mixed. Add the apple and hazelnuts and mix on low speed until evenly distributed.

Place the dough into an oiled rectangular container large enough for the dough to double in bulk. Cover with plastic wrap and set aside to rise for 20 minutes. Gently knock

(Continued overleaf.)

back the dough by folding it onto itself 2–3 times — use plenty of dusting flour in the container. Set aside to rest for a further 20 minutes.

Gently knock back the dough, again using plenty of dusting flour in the container. Set aside to rest for a further 20 minutes.

Repeat the knocking-back process, again using plenty of dusting flour in the container. Set aside to rest for a further 30 minutes. The dough should have firmed up.

Tip the dough onto a well-floured bench. Using a dough scraper, cut rectangles of dough in suitable sizes — remember it will increase in size by a third. Try to handle the dough as little as possible as rough handling will result in loss of air and gas bubbles. Loosely roll each rectangle in flour so that the top surface is covered with flour then place the pieces in a single layer on a well-floured tea towel with the floured surface up. Leave to rise for 45 minutes.

Pick up each dough piece and gently stretch it until it wants to spring back. Don't over-stretch it otherwise it will break and lose the gases trapped inside. Place them on a baking tray lined with non-stick baking paper. Slide the dough, still on the non-stick baking paper directly onto a baking stone or baking tray preheated to 230°C. Place in a preheated oven set at 230°C. Throw 4–5 ice cubes into a small ovenproof dish on the lower shelf. Quickly close the oven door.

Bake for 30–35 minutes until the crust is a dark golden brown colour and when the bottom is tapped the loaf sounds hollow. Remove from the oven and transfer to a cooling rack.

The dough once it is mixed in the mixing bowl.

Folding the dough to degas it, before allowing it to rise again.

Cutting the dough before placing it on a floured tea towel.

Stretching the dough onto the baking tray.

global baker baguette traditional

makes 4 baguettes

At Zarbo in Auckland and Baker & Spice in Shanghai our customers often tell us we make the best baguettes they have ever tasted. We don't use any special flours, preferring locally milled flours in New Zealand and China respectively. However, we do take special care throughout the process and one of the secrets is to keep the dough cold — even when going into the oven it should feel chilled. This results in open-textured bread that is bursting out of its crust.

dough

480g strong bread flour
20g wholemeal flour
100g levain (see page 221)
10g salt
5g malt flour (enzyme-active
    malt flour is best)
3g (¼ teaspoon) instant dried yeast

350ml chilled water (made by chilling
    the water down with ice cubes, taking
    care not to put the ice cubes into the
    dough)

additional flour for dusting
4–5 ice cubes for creating steam
    in the oven

Using a wooden spoon, mix all the ingredients together in a large mixing bowl to form a dough mass. Tip the dough out onto a lightly floured surface and knead for 10–15 minutes until the dough is smooth and elastic in feel. Take a rest period of 30 seconds every 2–3 minutes. Place the dough into a lightly oiled bowl large enough fot the dough to double in size and cover with lightly oiled plastic wrap. Leave in a warm place for 1 hour until almost doubled in size. Tip the dough onto the bench and knock back by folding it onto itself 3–4 times. Return the dough to the bowl and cover with plastic wrap. Set aside in a warm place for a further 30 minutes.

Gently tip the dough onto a lightly floured bench and divide into 4 equal pieces — 240g each. Flatten each piece of dough into a small rectangle then roll up into a tight Swiss roll. Form into baguette shapes 25–30cm long with tapered ends. Roll in flour and place seam-side down onto a tea towel that has been dusted with flour. Make a pleat of tea towel to separate each one, cover with a sheet of plastic wrap and set aside to rise for approximately 20 minutes until the dough is slightly active to the touch, but a little under-proofed.

Gently transfer each dough piece onto a baking tray lined with non-stick baking paper — you will need 2 baking trays. Lightly dust flour over the baguettes, if desired, then, using a sharp knife or razor blade, make 4 diagonal cuts across the top of each baguette.

Place the baking trays into a preheated oven set at 240°C, with a small ovenproof dish in the bottom shelf. Throw 4–5 ice cubes into the preheated ovenproof dish to make steam and quickly close the oven door. Bake for 15 minutes and then turn the trays around. Reduce the oven temperature to 200°C and bake for a further 10 minutes or until the crust is a dark golden brown colour and the loaves sound hollow when tapped on the bottom. Remove from the oven and transfer to a cooling rack.

fig & aniseed sourdough loaf

makes 5 small loaves

This has become one of our signature breads at Zarbo, because it's really good with a creamy blue cheese and a glass of your favourite wine or port.

500g strong bread flour

100g levain (see page 221)

20g whole aniseed, bruised with a mortar and pestle

10g salt

10g olive oil

2g instant dried yeast

320ml warm water

250g whole dried figs, hard stems removed, cut into 5–6 pieces

additional flour for dusting

4–5 ice cubes for creating steam in the oven

Mix the flour, levain, aniseed, salt, olive oil and yeast in a large mixing bowl until combined. Add the warm water. Using a wooden spoon, combine the ingredients until a dough mass has formed. Tip the dough out onto a lightly floured surface and knead for 10–15 minutes until the dough is smooth and elastic in feel. Take a rest period of 30 seconds every 2–3 minutes. Add the figs and gently knead until evenly distributed, taking care not to mash them up.

Place the dough into a lightly oiled bowl large enough for the dough to double in size and cover with lightly oiled plastic wrap. Leave in a warm place for approximately 1 hour until almost doubled in size. Tip the dough onto the bench and gently knock back by folding it onto itself 3–4 times. Return the dough to the lightly oiled bowl and cover with plastic wrap and set aside in a warm place for a further 30 minutes.

Tip the dough onto a lightly floured bench and divide into 5 equal pieces — 240g each. Flatten each piece of dough into a small rectangle and roll up into a tight Swiss roll then roll to form baguette shapes 25–30cm long with tapered ends. Roll in flour and place each dough piece seam-side down on a tea towel that has been dusted with flour. Make a pleat of tea towel to separate each one and cover with plastic wrap and set aside to rise for approximately 20 minutes until the dough is slightly active to the touch, but a little under-proofed.

Gently transfer each dough piece onto a baking tray lined with non-stick baking paper — you will need 2 baking trays. Lightly dust flour over the loaves, if desired, then, using a sharp knife or razor blade, make 4 diagonal cuts across the top of each loaf.

Place the baking trays into a preheated oven set at 240°C, with a small ovenproof dish in the bottom shelf. Throw 4–5 ice cubes into the preheated ovenproof dish to make steam and quickly close the oven door. Bake for 15 minutes and then turn the trays around. Reduce the oven temperature to 200°C and bake for a further 10 minutes or until the crust is a dark golden brown colour and the loaves sound hollow when tapped on the bottom. Remove from the oven and transfer to a cooling rack.

fruit & nut loaf

makes 1 loaf 10cm x 16cm

This breakfast fruit bread is packed with apricots, figs, cranberries and toasted almonds. The basic white dough with a hint of rye, orange zest and ground aniseed is not sweet, but the fruit provides plenty of natural sweetness. Cut thick slices of this loaf, toast them and serve with fresh butter — there's no need for anything else other than a cup of tea or coffee.

370g strong bread flour
30g rye flour
¼ teaspoon ground aniseed powder
8g (1½ teaspoons) salt
5g instant dried yeast
10g olive oil
zest of 1 orange
240ml water
75g dried apricots, cut into strips

75g whole dried figs, stems removed, chopped into 5 or 6 pieces
75g dried cranberries, roughly chopped
100g whole blanched almonds, lightly toasted and roughly chopped

additional flour for dusting
4–5 ice cubes for creating steam in the oven

Using a wooden spoon, mix the flours, aniseed, salt, yeast, olive oil, orange zest and water in a large bowl to form a dough mass. Tip the dough out onto a lightly floured surface and knead for 10–15 minutes until the dough is smooth and elastic in feel. Take a rest period of 30 seconds every 2–3 minutes.

Add the apricots, figs, cranberries and almonds and continue to knead until they they are evenly distributed, taking care not to mash the fruit.

Lightly oil a bowl large enough for the dough to double in size and put the dough in the bowl. Cover with lightly oiled plastic wrap and leave in a warm place (23–25°C) for 1 hour. Knock back the dough in the bowl by gently folding it back onto itself. Cover with plastic wrap and set aside for 30 minutes.

Tip the dough onto a lightly floured bench, flatten and mould into a rectangular loaf shape then place into a greased 10 x 16cm bread tin. Cover the loaf with plastic wrap and set aside to rise for 1–1 ½ hours depending on the room temperature until 1½ times in size.

Place into a preheated oven set at 190–200°C with a small ovenproof dish in the bottom shelf. Quickly throw the ice cubes into the ovenproof dish and bake for approximately 35–40 minutes until the loaf sounds hollow when tapped on the bottom. Remove from the oven and transfer to a cooling rack.

ultimate hot cross buns

makes 12 hot cross buns

Chances are these hot cross buns will be the best you have ever tasted. During Easter we cannot keep up with the demand at both Zarbo in Auckland and Baker & Spice in Shanghai. Trust me — they are so good you will be making more than one batch!

150g sultanas
100g currants
30ml rum
500g strong bread flour
3 tablespoons hot cross bun
   spice mix (see next page)
10g salt
40g butter
40g sugar

zest of 1 orange
10g instant dried yeast
1 egg
300ml water

additional flour for dusting
1 batch mixture for crosses
   (see next page)
1 batch sugar glaze (see next page)

Place the sultanas, currants and rum in a bowl and toss to ensure the fruit is evenly coated. Cover with plastic wrap and leave in a warm place overnight.

Using a wooden spoon, mix the remaining ingredients in a large bowl to form a dough mass. Tip the dough out onto a lightly floured surface and knead for 10–15 minutes until the dough is smooth and elastic in feel. Take a rest period of 30 seconds every 2–3 minutes. Don't be tempted to add excessive amounts of flour during the kneading process — but a little will be okay. Add the sultanas and currants and continue to knead until evenly distributed.

Lightly oil a bowl large enough for the dough to double in size and put the dough in the bowl. Cover with lightly oiled plastic wrap and leave in a warm place (23–25°C) for 45 minutes–1 hour. Remove the wrap and gently knock back the dough in the bowl by folding it back onto itself. Cover with the plastic wrap and set aside for 30 minutes.

Tip the dough onto a lightly floured bench and divide it into 12 equal pieces — 100g each. Roll each piece into a small ball or bun. Place buns 2cm apart on a baking tray or into a shallow, rectangular baking tin lined with non-stick baking paper. Cover with a sheet of plastic and allow to rise for 45 minutes–1 hour, depending on the room temperature. When the dough is pressed with the finger and it leaves an indentation in the dough, it is ready.

Place the mixture for crosses into a piping bag fitted with a 3mm plain piping nozzle (or use a plastic bag and cut a 3mm nip of the end with scissors) and pipe crosses onto the buns. Bake for 18–20 minutes in a preheated oven set at 180–190°C until golden brown.

While the buns are cooking, prepare the sugar glaze. Remove buns from the oven and brush with the sugar glaze and transfer them to a cooling rack.

(Continued overleaf.)

hot cross buns spice mix

2 teaspoons ground nutmeg

2 teaspoons ground ginger

2 teaspoons ground coriander

4 teaspoons ground cloves

6 teaspoons ground cinnamon

This makes enough for 2 batches. Mix all ingredients together and store in an airtight container until required.

mixture for crosses

75g plain flour

25g vegetable oil

75ml water

Place the flour and oil into a small bowl. Using a whisk, slowly mix together while adding the water in a steady stream. Whisk until a smooth and lump-free paste is formed. Cover with plastic wrap until required.

sugar glaze

100ml water

40g sugar

zest of 1 orange

Bring the water, sugar and zest to the boil. Remove from the heat and set aside until required.

dresdner christmas stollen

makes 2 large stollen

Thanks must go to Olaf, the head baker at Zarbo, for allowing me to share his grandmother's secret recipe with you. Stollen is a traditional Christmas fruit bread. Back in the fifteenth century, it was made without butter or milk because of a butter ban during Advent, and it was rather dull and dry. Fortunately for stollen's sake, the ban was lifted following an appeal to the Pope, and the rest is history. Make this stollen at least 1 month in advance to allow the flavour to mature, and serve, sliced, with a cup of coffee or tea.

fruit preparation

120g sultanas   30ml rum
120g currants

starter dough

75g milk, at room temperature   140g strong bread flour
6g instant dried yeast

stollen dough

1 batch starter dough   35ml milk
170g strong bread flour   3 x 40g pieces of butter
2 good pinches of salt   35g mixed peel
35g sugar   50g flaked almonds, lightly
⅛ teaspoon ground nutmeg   roasted in the oven at 170°C
¼ teaspoon ground cardamom   until amber in colour
1 vanilla pod, split lengthways,   300g good quality marzipan
    seeds scraped out and mixed
    with the milk

topping

150g unsalted butter   150g caster sugar for coating
70g icing sugar   extra icing sugar for dusting

Place the sultanas, currants and rum in a bowl and toss to ensure the fruit is evenly coated. Cover with plastic wrap and leave in a warm place overnight.

Place all the starter dough ingredients into a large mixing bowl and using a wooden spoon, mix until the dough has formed a mass, then place onto the bench and knead for 10 minutes until you have a smooth silky dough. Place into a lightly oiled bowl and cover with plastic wrap and allow to ferment for 30 minutes in a warm place.

(Continued overleaf.)

Now you are ready to make the stollen dough. Using a wooden spoon, mix the starter dough, flour, salt, sugar, nutmeg, cardamom, vanilla milk and 40g of butter together in a large bowl to form a dough mass. Tip the dough out onto a lightly floured surface and knead for approximately 5 minutes.

Add another 40g of butter and continue to knead until it is evenly distributed, then add the final portion of butter and knead until the dough is smooth and elastic in feel. This will take a while as the dough will be sticky to the touch, but don't be tempted to add excessive amounts of flour during the kneading process — but a little will be okay. Add the sultanas, currants, mixed peel and almonds and continue to knead gently until they are evenly distributed, taking care to avoid mashing the fruit.

Lightly oil a bowl large enough to allow the dough to double in size and put the dough in the bowl. Cover with lightly oiled plastic wrap and leave to rise in a warm place (23–25°C) for 45 minutes.

Divide the marzipan into 2 equal pieces and roll each piece into a sausage shape approximately 20cm long. Set aside until required.

Tip the dough onto a lightly floured bench and divide into 2 equal pieces — 450g each. Fold each piece into a rectangle and flatten with your hand. Place a marzipan sausage slightly off centre on each piece and fold over to enclose the marzipan. Using the handle of a wooden spoon, press firmly down on the dough along each side of the marzipan sausage to give the stollen its characteristic shape. Place on a baking tray lined with non-stick baking paper, cover with plastic wrap and leave to rise for 10 minutes. Bake for approximately 40–45 minutes in a preheated oven set at 180°C until golden brown in colour. Remove from the oven and cool for 20 minutes on a cooling rack.

To make the topping, melt the butter in a saucepan over a low heat. Add the icing sugar and whisk until smooth. Bring to the boil and then take off the heat. Dip each cooled stollen into the melted butter sugar mix, making sure it is completely submerged. Remove stollen from the liquid and return to the cooling rack to drain for 1 hour. Repeat the dipping process one more time and rest the stollen for 2–3 minutes before covering in caster sugar. Rest stollen overnight in a covered container or on a tray covered with a large plastic bag. Using a sieve, heavily dust the stollen with icing sugar and wrap individually in cellophane or plastic wrap for at least 4 weeks before cutting and eating.

savoury garden vegetable & cheese twist

makes 2 small twists or 1 large twist

I just love savoury scones and I couldn't go past the shape of a rustic plaited loaf as a change from the savoury pinwheel scones I grew up with. This is great served warm to bring out the savoury flavours and it goes well with a crisp apple cider.

filling

150g tasty cheddar cheese, grated
20g Parmesan cheese, grated
1 small egg
30g red onion, finely chopped
2 cloves garlic, crushed
25g red capsicum, finely chopped

25g green capsicum, finely chopped
2 tablespoons chopped fresh parsley
40g sun-dried tomato, finely chopped
40g olives, chopped
$1/2$ teaspoon smoked paprika
salt and pepper to taste

Mix all the ingredients together in a bowl to form a rough spreadable paste. Cover and set aside until required.

scone dough

380g plain flour
20g caster sugar
good pinch of salt
25g baking powder
70g butter, softened
1 egg

200ml milk

1 egg for egg wash
2 tablespoons water for egg wash
additional flour for dusting

Sift the flour, sugar, salt and baking powder into a large mixing bowl. Add the butter and rub into the flour using your fingertips and thumbs to form coarse crumbs. Whisk the egg and milk together and pour into the dry ingredients. Using a wooden spoon, mix together to form a soft dough. Tip the dough onto a floured bench and knead for 10–20 seconds — don't over-knead or the dough will become too elastic.

Cut the dough into 2 equal pieces or leave whole for a large loaf. Shape pieces of dough into squares. Using a rolling pin, roll out each dough piece on a floured bench to a 25cm square.

Whisk the egg and water together to make an egg wash.

Spread half the filling evenly on top of each dough sheet or all the filling over the single sheet of dough if making a large loaf, leaving about 1cm free along one edge. Brush egg wash along that edge. Working towards the edge painted with egg wash, firmly roll up each dough sheet to achieve a Swiss roll or log shape. Using a large chef's knife or dough scraper, make a single lengthways cut along the middle of each log, all the way through.

To make the log, take one strand in each hand with the cut side of each strand facing towards you and twist the strands around each other. Press the ends firmly together to make sure they do not unwind during the baking process. Place the twist onto a baking tray lined with non-stick baking paper, keeping them well apart so they don't join during baking. Brush the twist with remaining egg wash and allow to rest for 10 minutes. Bake smaller loaves for 30–35 minutes in a preheated oven set at 190–200°C. Turn the tray halfway through baking time to ensure an even colour. Remove from the oven and transfer to a cooling rack.

turkish pide

makes 6 small or 3 large loaves

Turkish bread is the new ciabatta and it's a superb way to make a sandwich without a chewy outer crust. The classic finish is a touch of egg wash and a light sprinkling of black sesame seeds. For a flavour hit I have added sun-dried tomato pesto and pesto verde, so making a sandwich is a whole lot easier — simply cut the loaf horizontally and fill with your favourite meats, salad or cheese.

dough

500g strong bread flour	360ml water
10g salt	
10g olive oil	1 egg for egg wash
10g sugar	50ml water for egg wash
5g instant dried yeast	additional flour for dusting

toppings

100g black sesame seeds (optional)	pesto verde (optional)
sun-dried tomato pesto (optional)	(see page 239)
(see page 241)	

Using a wooden spoon, mix the flour, salt, olive oil, sugar, yeast and water in a bowl to form a dough mass. Tip the dough out onto a lightly floured surface and knead for 10–15 minutes until the dough is smooth and elastic in feel. Take a rest period of 30 seconds every 2–3 minutes. The dough will be sticky to the touch, but don't be tempted to add excessive amounts of flour during the kneading process — but a little will be okay. Place the dough into a lightly oiled bowl large enough for the dough to double in size and cover with lightly oiled plastic wrap. Set aside to rise in a warm place for 1–1 ½ hours.

When the dough has doubled in size turn it out onto a floured surface and cut into pieces — 3 x 300g pieces for large and 6 x 150g for small pides. Very gently coax and stretch the dough pieces into oblong shapes, being careful not to knock too much gas out of the dough. Place the pieces on a floured bench and cover with plastic wrap. Allow to rest for 20 minutes. Place the pides 3–4cm apart on a baking tray lined with non-stick baking paper.

Whisk the egg and water together to make an egg wash and brush each pide with egg wash. Press your fingers firmly into the dough 5–6 times down the length of each loaf to make indentations. Sprinkle with sesame seeds or spread with sun-dried tomato pesto or pesto verde, if using. Set aside for a further 20 minutes to rise. Bake for 9–10 minutes in a preheated oven set at 250°C until almost motley in appearance with brown and white spots all over. The pesto-topped pides will take a little longer to bake. Remove from the oven and transfer to a cooling rack.

olaf's vollkorn loaf

makes 1 loaf 10cm x 16cm

Olaf Blanke, the head baker at Zarbo, hails from Germany. It was only natural that he wanted a loaf of bread full of grains on the shelf. Although it's not one of our biggest sellers, it's there for the many Europeans who come to find a taste of their homeland and they are not disappointed. Olaf's loaf is full of rye grains and has a very dense and solid crumb that goes well with cold cuts and cheese.

seed mix

250g kibbled rye

50g pumpkin seeds

50g sunflower seeds

250g hot water

Place all the seed mix ingredients in a bowl and stir together. Cover and soak overnight at room temperature.

dough

60g strong bread flour

200g rye flour

60g rye meal

225g rye sourdough levain
  (see page 221)

5g gluten flour

10g salt

7g instant dried yeast (1 sachet)

15g molasses

5g caraway seeds, lightly bruised
  with a mortar and pestle

additional flour for dusting

30g pumpkin seeds for topping

30g sunflower seeds for topping

3–4 ice cubes for creating steam
  in the oven

Place all the ingredients, including the soaked grains and seeds, into the bowl of an electric mixer fitted with a dough hook. Mix for 2 minutes on slow speed then scrape down the bowl and hook. The mixture will be more like a stiff biscuit dough than a soft bread dough. Mix for a further 3 minutes on slow–medium speed.

Scrape the dough onto a floured bench and mould into a tight oblong sausage-shaped cylinder.

Roll the dough shape in water and then in the pumpkin and sunflower seeds and place in a lightly oiled 10 x 16cm loaf tin (or a non-stick loaf tin). Cover very loosely with plastic wrap and leave at room temperature overnight until the dough has risen almost to the height of the tin. Place into a preheated oven set at 250°C with a small ovenproof dish in the bottom shelf. Quickly throw ice cubes into the ovenproof dish to make steam and bake for 5 minutes and then turn the oven down to 190°C.

Bake for 1 hour or until the loaf sounds hollow when tapped on the bottom. Transfer to a cooling rack.

beetroot, pumpkin, feta & roasted garlic focaccia-style quick bread

makes 2 rustic loaves

When time is short I love to make a batch of quick bread to serve with a hearty winter soup or freshly cooked fillet of fish with a crisp green salad. All quick breads are best eaten within a few hours of baking.

500g bread flour
5g salt
40g baking powder
good pinch of freshly ground
   black pepper
1 tablespoon chopped thyme
1 tablespoon chopped rosemary
65g unsalted butter, softened
380ml tepid milk

150g feta cheese, roughly cut into small
   cubes
150g pumpkin cubes, partly cooked
   in the microwave
150g beetroot cubes, partly cooked
   in the microwave
flesh squeezed from 1 bulb roasted
   garlic (see page 99)

topping
sprigs carefully removed from
   1 stalk of rosemary

6 cherry tomatoes, cut in half

Sift the flour, salt, baking powder and and pepper into a large bowl and add the chopped herbs. Add the softened butter and using your fingertips and thumbs, rub the butter into the dry ingredients until they resemble breadcrumbs. Make a large well in the centre and slowly add the milk. Gently mix the ingredients to form a dough mass, taking care not to over-mix. Once the dough is almost combined but it still has wet and floury patches throughout, add the remaining ingredients, folding and lifting them through the dough until evenly distributed. Do not over-mix or the resulting loaf will be tough.

Divide the dough into 2 equal parts and very lightly shape each into an oblong shape. With the smooth side facing up, place each dough piece onto a baking tray lined with non-stick baking paper. Using the palm of your hand, gently flatten each piece to 3cm thick and dust with white flour. Poke the halved cherry tomatoes and rosemary sprigs into the surface of each loaf. Using a large knife or dough scraper, cut a deep trellis pattern into each loaf taking care not to cut all the way through. Set aside to rest in a cool place for 15 minutes.

Bake for 20–25 minutes in a preheated oven set at 220°C until golden brown in colour and sounding hollow when the bottom is tapped. Remove from the oven and transfer to a cooling rack.

cinnamon & pecan easter quick bread twist

makes 2 small twists or 1 large twist

This is perfect for those people who don't like traditional hot cross buns with all those dried sultanas and currants. It's quick and easy to make and looks attractive. The icing adds a sweet touch to the lovely flavours of the spices.

cinnamon filling

85g flour

50g brown sugar

2 teaspoons ground cinnamon

$\frac{1}{2}$ teaspoon of mixed spice

$1\frac{1}{2}$ tablespoons butter, softened

2 egg whites

$\frac{3}{4}$ cup pecans, toasted and chopped

Using a wooden spoon, mix the flour, sugar, cinnamon, mixed spice and butter in a large bowl to form a coarse crumb. Add the egg whites, half an egg white at a time, and mix well after each addition. Scrape down the sides of the bowl if necessary. The mixture should be soft and smooth with a nice spreading consistency, not too runny. Set aside until required.

scone dough

380g plain flour

60g caster sugar

25g baking powder

good pinch of salt

70g butter, softened

1 egg

190ml milk

1 egg for egg wash

2 tablespoons water for egg wash

apricot glaze, heated (see page 242)

white icing (see page 245)

Sift together the flour, sugar, baking powder and salt into a large bowl. Add the butter and rub into the flour using your finger tips and thumbs to form fine crumbs. Whisk the egg and milk together and pour into the dry ingredients. Using a wooden spoon, mix together to form a soft dough. Tip the dough out onto a floured bench and knead for 10–20 seconds — don't over-knead at this stage or the dough will become too elastic.

Cut into 2 equal pieces or leave whole for a large loaf. Using a rolling pin, roll out each dough piece on a lightly floured bench to a 25cm square. Whisk the egg and water together to make an egg wash.

Spread half the filling evenly on top of each square or all the filling over one square if making a large loaf, leaving a 1cm strip free along one edge. Brush egg wash along that edge. Working towards the edge painted with egg wash, firmly roll up each square to form a Swiss roll or log. Using a large chef's knife or dough scraper, make a single lengthways cut along the middle of each log all the way through.

For each log, take one strand in each hand with the cut side of each strand facing up and twist the strands around each other. Press the ends firmly together to make sure they do not unwind during the baking process. Place the twists on a baking tray lined with non-stick baking paper keeping them well apart so they don't join during baking. Brush the twists with the remaining egg wash and set aside to rest for 10 minutes. Bake for 30–35 minutes for small loaves or 35–40 minutes for a large loaf in a preheated oven set at 190–200°C. Turn the tray halfway through baking to ensure an even colour. Remove from the oven and brush immediately with hot apricot glaze. Transfer to a cooling rack and when cool use a pastry brush to brush white icing all over the twists.

the ultimate muesli breakfast scone

makes 12 scones

When I feel like a scone and a piping hot café latte to pick me up, this is the one that hits the spot. It's chock full of goodness with seeds, oats, fruit, nuts and fresh orange purée. It's delicious served just warm and there's no need to add butter because there is already a good amount in the recipe. The streusel topping is the icing on the cake!

oaty streusel topping

100g brown sugar

40g flour

¼ teaspoon cinnamon

40g butter, softened

1 teaspoon water

100g jumbo rolled oats

Mix the sugar, flour and cinnamon together in a bowl. Add the butter and mix until just combined but not creamy. Add the water and rolled oats and mix by hand until a mixture of pea-sized crumbs is formed. Set aside until required.

scone dough

50g jumbo rolled oats

50g sunflower seeds

30g pumpkin seeds

20g sesame seeds

20g flax or linseeds

15g aniseed, ground in a pestle and mortar to release the flavours

50g warm water

350g plain flour

10g baking powder

1g baking soda

¼ teaspoon cinnamon

5g salt

215g butter, at room temperature

85g sugar

10g honey

1 egg

50g orange (including rind, pith and flesh), blended to make a purée

80ml milk

50g figs, stalks removed, cut into small pieces

50g dried cranberries

80g apricots, chopped

20g thread coconut, lightly toasted until golden

70g whole natural almonds, roughly chopped

1 egg

2 tablespoons water

Mix the rolled oats, sunflower seeds, pumpkin seeds, sesame seeds, flax seeds, aniseed and warm water together in a bowl, ensuring all the grains and seeds are coated with water. Set aside for at least 30 minutes.

Sift the flour, baking powder, baking soda, cinnamon and salt into a bowl and set aside until required. Combine the butter, sugar and honey in the bowl of an electric mixer fitted with a beater and mix until light and creamy. Scrape down the mixing bowl and add the dry ingredients and continue mixing on low speed for 2 minutes. Add the egg, orange purée and milk and mix on low speed for 2 minutes and then add the soaked grains, dried fruit, coconut and chopped nuts. Mix for a further 2 minutes until the dough is smooth.

Tip the dough onto a lightly floured bench and divide into 3 equal pieces — 400g each. Flour the bench again and form each piece into a round shape then flatten to a 12–15cm diameter circle. Transfer each circle to a plate and cover with plastic wrap. Put in the refrigerator for 1–2 hours or overnight to firm up.

When ready to bake, remove from the refrigerator then, using a large knife, cut each circle of scone dough into quarters. Separate each quarter and place 2 cm apart on a baking tray lined with non-stick baking paper. Whisk the egg and water together to make an egg wash and brush the top of each scone. Sprinkle the oaty streusel topping evenly over the scones and bake for 25–30 minutes in a preheated oven set at 200°C. Remove from the oven and transfer to a cooling rack.

entrées

entrées

There were a number of different reasons for choosing recipes for this chapter. Some are perfect dinner party entrées, others are ideal as a Sunday brunch or supper. Some of the salads can be served either as a side dish or made into a full meal with the addition of some great bread from the bakery. A number of these dishes are also suitable to be shared as part of a picnic. Many can be made in advance and stored — in some cases for quite a few weeks.

Flicking through a big glossy cookbook from the 1980s recently, I noted the complexity of some of the dishes and how structured the menus were. If nothing else, this would have led to a lot of stress for the host. Fortunately, our approach to entertaining has changed dramatically since then and the dishes in this chapter reflect that change. For most of us now, the heart of the home is the kitchen and entertaining is much more casual. Eating times are also more flexible.

When we are entertaining I do all the cooking — the type of food that I have included here — and Cushla makes sure that everybody's wine glass is kept full. I prepare most courses well in advance and serve them as platters so guests can help themselves. Guests are then free to choose what they want to eat and how much they want to eat. This also deals with any special dietary needs that people may have — one of the other big changes that I have noticed in recent years is the increase in the number of people with allergies and various forms of food intolerance.

My wish is that you have fun trying out these recipes and that they become firm favourites in your culinary repertoire.

the cook

salmon tartare

serves 4 as a casual brunch or 6 as an entrée

I love the richness of salmon and when it's fresh this is one recipe I like to use. There is a bit of effort in dicing the salmon but it's worth it. I have included chopped cooked egg whites for contrast of colour and also texture. This is great served elegantly as a dinner party entrée — it can also be shaped using a mould — but is equally good for a casual weekend brunch served with some crusty bread. Made in advance, it can be refrigerated for up to 4 hours before serving.

400g fresh salmon, deboned
2 anchovy fillets (optional)
6 cornichons, finely diced
6 teaspoons capers
1 tablespoon finely diced onion
$\frac{1}{4}$ cup dill
cooked whites of 3 eggs
grated rind of 1 lemon
salt and pepper to taste

Using a very sharp knife, skin and very finely slice the salmon. Place in a bowl.

Very finely dice the anchovy, if using, cornichons, capers and onion. Add to the salmon.

Roughly chop the dill and the egg white and add to the mix. Add the lemon rind and season with salt and pepper.

Using your hands stir the mixture well to combine. Cover with plastic wrap and refrigerate for a minimum of 2 hours. Divide evenly over 4 or 6 plates, as required.

asian lettuce cups

serves 4

This is my adaptation of a dish that my wife, Cushla, and I always order when we go to our favourite local Chinese restaurant in Newmarket. It is so easy to prepare at home and although it can be a bit messy to eat it tastes sensational. I have used beef schnitzel finely diced for this, however very lean mince is also acceptable. Take care when peeling the leaves from the lettuce as they are delicate and do tend to rip easily. This is a great dish to share.

1 small onion, finely diced
1 tablespoon minced ginger
4 cloves garlic, finely diced
a little sesame oil
400g schnitzel, finely diced
green bits of 4 spring onions, finely sliced
1 cup bean sprouts, chopped
⅓ cup hoisin sauce
2 tablespoons black bean sauce
20 lettuce cups
extra hoisin sauce for serving

Sauté the onion, ginger and garlic in the sesame oil until aromatic. Add the beef and brown. Fold through the spring onion, bean sprouts, hoisin and black bean sauce and cook through.

Serve in a bowl with the lettuce cups on the side and allow your guests to spoon some of the mix into a lettuce cup before folding and dipping into a dish of hoisin sauce.

middle eastern platter

serves 6–20, depending on the occasion

A real crowd pleaser, this platter takes a bit of effort but your family and guests will love it. Serve it with plenty of bread and you are onto a real winner. This dish is a meal in itself — it's great as a lunch, a light al fresco dinner or packed for a picnic. It can be a meal for six or it can be an entrée for 20 — simply pile the platter high and start partying.

The labne, marinated olives and pickled cucumbers will all last a couple of weeks in your fridge.

labne

1 litre good quality full-fat unsweetened natural yoghurt
juice of ½ a lemon
¾ teaspoon salt
1 tablespoon dried mint
pinch of cracked pepper

Put all the ingredients in a bowl and stir to combine. Line another bowl with muslin and pour in the yoghurt mix. Pull the edges of the muslin together to form a ball and tie with some string. Suspend the ball over a container for a minimum of 24 hours and up to 48 hours in a cool dark place — not the refrigerator — until all excess liquid has drained. Transfer to the refrigerator for 24 hours to set. Roll into small balls and use, or layer them in a sterilised jar and cover with olive oil. They will keep for several weeks in the refrigerator.

lamb kofta

1 medium onion, finely diced
4 cloves garlic, finely diced
1kg lean lamb mince
1 teaspoon zaartar
1 cup chopped mint
½ cup chopped flat-leaf parsley
salt and pepper

Put all the ingredients in a bowl and squish together. Roll into small ovals. Thread onto bamboo skewers that have been soaked in cold water for 20 minutes and cook under a preheated grill or on a barbecue grill rack for 3–5 minutes on each side until cooked through.

(Continued overleaf.)

marinated kalamata olives

Place olives, some garlic cloves and some toasted cumin and fennel seeds in a roasting dish. Drizzle on a little olive oil and toss to combine. Roast in an oven preheated to 180°C until the olives have just begun to wrinkle. Remove from oven and once cool transfer to a sterilised jar with fresh orange segments. Cover with good quality olive oil, seal and store in a cool, dark place until required.

pickled cucumber

500g whole baby cucumbers (the sort you buy in packs of 5)
2 cloves garlic, crushed
½ cup fresh dill leaves
2 teaspoons black peppercorns
500ml water
100ml white vinegar
1 tablespoon salt

Wash cucumbers well and pat dry with paper towels. Arrange the cucumber, garlic, dill and peppercorns in layers in sterilised jars. Combine the water, vinegar and salt in a saucepan and bring to the boil. Pour over the cucumbers then seal the jars and let stand at room temperature for at least 10 days.

italian blanched squid

serves 4

This simple squid salad is great for an entrée or served as part of a selection of salads. The key to this dish is to have the sauce ready before you quickly blanch and drain the squid.

6 squid tubes
zest and juice of 6 lemons
$\frac{1}{4}$ cup chopped dill
$\frac{1}{4}$ cup chopped flat-leaf parsley
olive oil
1 chilli, deseeded and finely diced (to taste)
1 tablespoon capers
500ml boiling water
sea salt and cracked pepper

Finely slice the squid tubes. Combine the lemon zest, juice, dill, parsley, olive oil, chilli and capers.

Blanch the squid for just a few seconds in boiling water, remove, drain and immediately drop into the prepared sauce. Stir to combine and season to taste.

chicken, bacon & corn soup

serves 6

Soups are always popular. I make this simple, easily prepared soup when fresh corn is available, but frozen corn is just about as good. I like to make soups a day in advance to allow the flavour to develop. Most soups freeze well and I will often make a soup to freeze in individual serving-sized pots for my wife to take to work for lunch.

1 large onion, diced
4 cloves garlic crushed, peeled and roughly diced
6 rashers lean bacon, diced
olive oil
400g chicken thigh meat, diced
1 teaspoon Spanish sweet smoked paprika
2 litres chicken stock
4 cups fresh corn kernels cut off the cob
salt and pepper
2 handfuls of baby spinach leaves

Put the onion, garlic and bacon and a little olive oil in a frying pan and sauté until tender. Add the chicken and sauté until browned on all sides. Add the paprika and stir to combine. Pour in the stock and add 2 cups of the corn. Bring to the boil, reduce the heat and simmer for 20 minutes. Add the remaining corn, season to taste and simmer for a further 10 minutes. Finally add the spinach and cook for a further 5 minutes.

mediterranean green bean salad

serves 6

A stunning salad to serve on a platter, use whatever beans are in season. I like to blanch the beans then refresh them in iced water to halt the cooking process — and to help them retain their colour.

A salad like this does not really need a dressing — there is enough flavour in the basic ingredients. However, if you aren't serving this immediately you might like to splash over a little olive oil to freshen it before serving.

600g assorted beans, trimmed but left whole
2 bunches asparagus, ends removed
2 cups broad beans
150g feta, crumbled
$\frac{1}{2}$ cup sun-dried tomatoes
$\frac{1}{2}$ cup kalamata olives
$\frac{1}{2}$ cup balsamic baby onions

Steam the beans or blanch them in boiling water and refresh in iced water. Set aside until required.

Chargrill the asparagus on a barbecue hotplate or in a lightly oiled grill pan and set aside to cool.

Blanch the broad beans and peel.

Combine the beans, asparagus and broad bean kernels on a platter. Sprinkle over the feta, sun-dried tomatoes, olives and baby onions.

insalata caprese

serves 4 as a side dish

This is it — a real classic. The best Capreses that I have ever eaten were along the Amalfi Coast and on the island of Capri in Italy. I'm not sure if it was because of the freshness of the cheese and basil, the quality of the sun-ripened tomatoes, or the romanticism of sitting in a rustic trattoria with family enjoying great food and great wine. For best results, use the best ingredients available.

250g Italian buffalo mozzarella
4–6 ripe beefsteak tomatoes
a generous handful of fresh basil leaves, freshly picked
very good quality extra virgin olive oil
freshly cracked pepper and sea salt

Slice the mozzarella and the tomatoes and layer on a plate with the basil.

Drizzle over the olive oil and season with salt and pepper to taste.

avocado, grapefruit salad with gazpacho dressing

serves 4

This is a nice flavoursome salad for summer. There is a bit of work involved in dicing everything for the Gazpacho dressing, but it is worth the effort to achieve the texture. Prepare the grapefruit and avocado just before serving and gently fold through the rocket so that the avocado retains it firmness.

salad

2 avocados, destoned, peeled and cubed

2 grapefruit, all peel and pith removed, segmented

2 cups rocket

dressing

1 clove garlic, finely diced

1/4 cup cucumber, finely diced

1 red capsicum, finely diced

1 large tomato, deseeded and finely diced

generous handful of fresh basil leaves

2 tablespoons sherry vinegar

3 tablespoons olive oil

squeeze of lemon juice

splash of chilli sauce (optional)

pinch of sugar

salt and pepper

Put all the dressing ingredients in a screw-top jar and shake to combine. Season to taste with pepper and salt. Combine salad ingredients in a bowl or on a platter and gently toss the dressing through the salad.

chilled avocado, lime & cucumber soup

serves 4

This soup does have a bit of an 1980s thing going on but, with the benefit of hindsight, it feels all right to go back there. Chilled soups are a refreshing summer treat. This soup needs to be made with a fresh, clean, green stock — not a brown stock. Make the stock the day before so it is chilled before you begin. The diced cucumber folded through at the end adds an appealing texture.

green vegetable stock

5–6 cups water
½ a small white onion
2 courgettes

a few green beans
handful of fresh basil leaves

Place all the ingredients in a large stockpot and bring to the boil. Reduce the heat and simmer for 30 minutes. Remove from the heat and strain the liquid into a clean bowl. Allow to cool and transfer to the refrigerator to chill until required — I suggest making this a day in advance.

soup

3 large ripe avocados, destoned and peeled
juice of 3 limes or more to taste
4 cups green vegetable stock, at room temperature (see above)
1 cup yoghurt

½ a large cucumber peeled, deseeded and finely diced
salt and pepper to taste
1 small red chilli, deseeded and finely diced (optional)

Put the avocado flesh into a food processor and blend. Add the lime juice and 2 cups of the stock. Pulse to combine. Add the remaining stock and pulse to combine. Add the yoghurt and combine.

Remove from the food processor and transfer to a bowl. Fold through the cucumber and season with salt and pepper. Adjust seasoning, adding extra lime juice if required.

Transfer to individual serving bowls and garnish with chopped chilli, if using.

winter vegetable soup with israeli couscous and borlotti beans

serves 4

This is a hearty winter soup that's great as an entrée but because of the beans and couscous, served with some grilled bread, it is also excellent as a simple Sunday night dinner. Wild Italian oregano is available from speciality food stores.

1 large onion, diced
4 cloves garlic, crushed
olive oil
4 courgettes, roughly chopped
1 cup white wine
4 anchovy fillets (optional)
1 x 400g tin whole peeled tomatoes,
    hand crushed

2 teaspoons wild Italian oregano
2 cups green vegetable stock
    (see page 80)
1 $\frac{1}{2}$ litres water
$\frac{1}{2}$ cup Israeli couscous
$\frac{1}{2}$ cup borlotti beans, soaked
    overnight and cooked
salt and pepper

Put the onion and garlic and a little olive oil in a large stockpot and sauté until transparent. Add the courgettes and stir. Pour in the wine to deglaze the pan then add the anchovies, if using, and tomatoes and stir in the oregano. Next add the stock, water, couscous and borlotti beans. Season with salt and pepper. Bring to the boil, reduce heat and simmer for 40 minutes.

beef carpaccio with basil caper purée

serves 4

This is a restaurant entrée that I believe is quite achievable at home. The key is to slice the beef as thinly as possible using a very sharp knife. Freezing the meat first makes this easy to do. The recipe calls for 400g of meat, but I like to use a piece that is 800g–1kg — that way I'm less likely to cut myself.

I blend the dressing as finely as possible and transfer it to a squirty bottle for ease of pouring over the beef. You can also use this method to make a carpaccio of tuna.

400g scotch fillet, with core of fat
   removed
1 clove garlic, peeled
2 cups basil leaves, blanched,
   refreshed in iced water, and
   squeezed to remove excess water

2 teaspoons capers
80ml best quality olive oil
1 teaspoon lemon juice

Wrap the beef in plastic wrap and freeze until firm, but not solid.

In a food processor, blend the garlic, basil and capers then slowly pour in the olive oil and lemon juice to form a smooth dressing.

Remove the beef from the freezer and slice as thinly as possible. Arrange slices neatly on 4 serving plates. Gently squirt or pour the purée over the beef and serve immediately.

oysters three ways

serves 6

Growing up in Southland, for me pigging out on Bluff oysters was a regular event. I remember my father bringing home huge sacks full and everyone sitting around shucking them and eating them straight from their shells. The most anybody thought to add, if pressed, was a dribble of malt vinegar. Back then, if you'd suggested three ways of preparing oysters people would have thought you were from Mars. I like to serve this as a tasting plate.

spanish style

18 Bluff oysters
1 cup white wine
2 tablespoons cardamom pods
1 teaspoon Spanish sweet smoked paprika
1 teaspoon cardamom seeds, toasted
   and crushed with a mortar and pestle

Put all the ingredients in a small saucepan and bring to the boil. Remove from the heat and strain the liquid. Allow to cool and chill in the refrigerator until required.

japanese style

80ml Japanese soy sauce
juice of 2 limes
2 tablespoons toasted sesame seeds
18 Bluff oysters

Combine the soy and lime juice and add the toasted sesame seeds. Set aside the remaining sesame seeds to sprinkle over the dressed oysters.

italian style

18 Bluff oysters
2 tablespoons capers, drained
olive oil
80ml grappa
½ tomato deseeded, membrane removed, very finely sliced
1 teaspoon very finely chopped flat-leaf parsley

Place the drained capers on a couple of paper towels and squeeze out any excess brine. Heat a little olive oil in a frying pan, add the capers and fry for a couple of minutes. Remove from the pan and drain on paper towels until cool.

To serve, arrange 2 oysters in their half shell on a mound of crushed ice in the middle of each serving plate. Drizzle a little of the Spanish-style sauce over one oyster on each plate and a little of the Japanese-style sauce over the other oyster. For the Italian-style, pour the grappa into 6 shot glasses and drop an oyster into each. Top with tomato and parsley and stir gently. Finally, drop in a few of the fried capers.

duck terrine

serves 6

Terrines are a classic dish but many people are put off making them because they consider it too difficult, but the truth is they are very easy to prepare and cook. Aaron, the photographer for this book, and I had some fun styling this dish. This is the first project that we have worked on together and this grey and visually unappealing terrine was the first dish I gave him to photograph — as you can see he got it just right.

2 duck breasts
200g pork belly
150g chicken livers
100g streaky bacon
10 allspice berries
100ml white wine
50ml cognac
3 cloves garlic, crushed and roughly chopped
a little anchovy oil
salt and pepper
extra fat for sealing the surface, if required

Cut all the meat into very fine pieces and place in a large bowl. Crush the allspice berries with a mortar and pestle and add to the meat mix. Add wine, cognac, garlic, anchovy oil and season with salt and pepper. Mix well until thoroughly combined.

Divide the mixture evenly between 6 ramekins and cover tightly with foil. Place into a high sided pan then fill with boiling water to come halfway up the sides of the ramekins. Carefully place in a preheated oven set at 160°C and cook for $1\frac{3}{4}$ hours. Remove foil and cook for a further 5 minutes. Remove from the oven and when cool, pour melted fat onto the surface of each terrine to make an airtight seal. Cover with plastic and place in the refrigerator overnight or until required. They will keep in the refrigerator for several weeks.

To serve, crack and carefully remove the sealing fat and serve with crostini or a crusty French stick.

poached peaches with prosciutto & gorgonzola

serves 6

I ordered this as an entrée on a recent family holiday in Australia. The flavours and textures were wonderful and I have since made it many times. The kids enjoy it minus the gorgonzola.

600g fresh peaches (soft but still with a bit of crispness)
150g finely sliced prosciutto, torn into pieces
100g gorgonzola, crumbled

Depending upon the firmness of the peaches there are two ways of preparing them. Cut peaches into quarters and remove the stones. Cut into bite-sized slices. If the peaches are soft, sprinkle with a little sugar and cook on a preheated barbecue hotplate or under a grill. If the peaches are firm blanch the slices quickly in boiling water before sprinkling with sugar.

Arrange the peaches on a plate with the torn prosciutto and using your fingers, fold to combine and make a pile. Take care to get a bit of height into the pile. Sprinkle the crumbled gorgonzola cheese on top and serve immediately.

two dips

each dip makes 3 cups

This is the sort of food I prepare when we have friends over for a drink on a lazy summer afternoon. Both dips are easy to prepare and, with grilled crostini, they create a platter full of contrasting colours and texture.

goat's cheese, spinach & parsley dip

3–4 large bunches spinach

2 cloves chopped garlic

¼ cup chopped parsley

200g goat's cheese, crumbled

a pinch of nutmeg

a pinch of ground cumin

2 cups cottage cheese

To prepare the spinach, remove the stalks and blanch the leaves in boiling water. Refresh in iced water to maintain the colour. When cool, remove from the water and, using your hands, squeeze out as much of the excess water as possible. Roughly chop the spinach and pack into a measuring cup — you will need 1 tightly packed cup of blanched spinach.

Place spinach, garlic, parsley and crumbled goat's cheese in a food processor and process until combined — you may need to scrape down the sides of the bowl from time to time. Add the nutmeg and cumin and process to mix through. Add the cottage cheese and very gently pulse to just combine all the ingredients. Do not over blend — you want to retain the texture of the cottage cheese. You may prefer to fold the cottage cheese through by hand.

sun-dried tomato, black olive & anchovy dip

2 cups sun-dried tomatoes, drained

1 cup kalamata olives, pitted

12 anchovies (more or less to taste)

2 tablespoons capers

a little olive oil, if required

cracked pepper

Roughly chop the tomatoes on a board then place into a food processor and process until smooth. Add the olives, anchovies and capers and blend retaining some texture, but adding olive oil if necessary. Season with cracked pepper.

prawn, chilli & vietnamese-mint pot stickers

serves 6

With the dipping sauce on the side, these make an easy and impressive entrée. Virtually any meat or vegetable can be used if prawns are not to your liking.

pot stickers

175g prawn meat, diced
1 small red chilli
8–10 sprigs Vietnamese mint
1 clove garlic
1 teaspoon freshly minced ginger
1 tablespoon sesame oil

1 tablespoon light soy sauce
1 ½ teaspoons cornflour
black pepper
24 dim sim wrappers
peanut oil for frying
1 cup vegetable stock or water

Put the prawn meat, chilli, mint, garlic, ginger, sesame oil, soy sauce, cornflour and a good grind of black pepper in a bowl and mix together until well combined.

Lay the dim sim wrappers on a clean work surface. Place 1 teaspoon of the prawn mixture into the centre of each wrapper. One at a time, brush the edges of the wrappers with a little water and fold over the mixture to make a parcel. Squeeze the edges tightly to seal.

Heat a little oil in a shallow frying pan large enough to arrange all the pot stickers in a single layer. When the oil is hot put the pot stickers in the pan and cook until browned on the underside. Add the stock or water and steam until the pot stickers are cooked through.

dipping sauce

2 kaffir lime leaves
2 tablespoons black vinegar
2 tablespoons Japanese soy

2 tablespoons fish sauce
juice of 1 lemon
1 tablespoon grated palm sugar

Mix all the ingredients together until well combined.

chicken tenders with panko & smoked paprika aïoli

serves 6–12, depending on the occasion

Panko crumbs come from Japan and are now readily available from Asian supermarkets, most delis and some supermarkets. I use them in meatballs as well as for coating pieces of fish and chicken.

The key to this dish is the double coating of crumbs that gives the chicken a nice crisp finish.

I serve this as a platter with a simple dipping sauce when we have people over for a beer and it is just as popular with the kids. It's just as good served cold and will travel well to a picnic. Leftovers also make a great addition to school lunchboxes.

4 eggs
¼ cup milk
salt and pepper
24 chicken tenderloins left whole or 5 chicken breasts, each sliced into 5 strips
2 cups panko crumbs
grapeseed oil for frying

Whisk the eggs and milk together. Season with salt and pepper and stir to combine.

Dip the chicken pieces one at a time in the egg mix then roll in panko crumbs until well coated. Repeat the process, making the sure the chicken is well and evenly coated. Place on a sheet of baking paper.

Heat a little oil in a frying pan and brown the tenderloins on all sides then drain on paper towels. You will need to do this in a few batches so the oil maintains its heat.

Place all the tenderloins in a preheated baking dish and finish off in a preheated oven set at 160°C for 10 minutes or until cooked through — when pierced the juices will be clear.

smoked sweet paprika aïoli

This is moreish and can be used as a dip or dressing as a change from plain mayo.

4 egg yolks
1 clove garlic, finely diced
1½ teaspoons smoked sweet Spanish paprika
1½ cups olive oil
salt and pepper

Put the egg yolks, garlic and paprika in a food processor and blend until smooth. Very slowly drip the olive oil down the feeder tube with the machine running on low speed until a thick and creamy mayonnaise is formed. Season to taste and store in the refrigerator in an airtight container until required.

marinated chargrilled capsicums

serves 4 as an entrée or as many as part of an antipasti platter

Once, when I told one of our regular customers that I was making this dish, she asked me to save some for her. She was stoked and loved the taste. I often throw a bulb or two of garlic into the oven when I'm cooking a roast to have ready for simple dishes like this.

A dish we would serve from our deli counter, it also looks great on an antipasti platter and makes a delicious pizza topping.

selection of brightly coloured capsicums
2 bulbs garlic
olive oil
sea salt and pepper
chopped fresh thyme for garnish
chopped fresh rosemary for garnish

Cook the capsicums under a grill or over a barbecue grill preheated to a medium heat. Turn them over and continue cooking until all the skins are blistered and blackened. Transfer them to a bowl and cover with plastic wrap. When cooled, peel off all the blackened skin and remove the core and seeds. Tear the flesh into strips.

While the capsicums are cooking, chop the root end from the bulb of garlic and discard. Rub the bulb with a little olive oil and sprinkle with sea salt. Place in a preheated oven set at 180°C and roast for 40–45 minutes. Remove from the oven and set aside to cool.

Arrange the capsicum flesh in a bowl and squeeze the roasted garlic flesh from the cloves into the bowl — much like squeezing toothpaste from a tube. Sprinkle the herbs over and drizzle a little extra oil over the top and gently toss to combine. Just before serving, season with salt and pepper.

traditional potted cheese

serves 8 as an entrée or many as part of an antipasti platter

Yummy and rich to serve as an entrée or to take on a picnic, this works with pretty much any combination of cheeses — just make sure you have 350g in total. Wrapped in foil, this will last for several weeks in your fridge, as long as you can resist it.

175g cheddar (I like to use a sharp English cheddar)
125g blue cheese (I like to use a creamy French blue)
50g St Nectaire (if unavailable, use a firm Camembert or Brie)
2 tablespoons butter, softened
2 tablespoons crème fraîche
freshly ground black pepper
2 tablespoons freshly snipped chives
oil

Crumble the cheeses into a bowl, add the butter, créme fraîche, pepper and chives. Using your fingers, mix everything together — make sure that some texture is retained.

Oil a sheet of tin foil and roughly make the cheese mixture into a log. Place the log onto the foil and roll the foil over the log to make it airtight. Continue rolling the log on a bench to form a nice even shape. Square off the ends. Refrigerate for several hours or overnight until required.

main meals

main meals

While the dishes in this chapter will take a little bit more effort they are definitely achievable by the home cook. I try to make my dishes as user-friendly as possible and over the years I have been pleased by the number of people who have told me that they find my recipes both practical and useful. I also like to introduce a few new ingredients and or cooking methods to inspire people and give them the confidence to experiment and try new things in the kitchen. It is not rocket science — it's home cooking and it's meant to be fun!

As most of us are working long hours it can be challenging to cook each night but with a little organisation it is not difficult to put an easy nutritious meal on the table relatively quickly. Week nights, I aim to cook things that can be prepared in 20–30 minutes — some are ready to eat and some are then thrown into the oven to cook.

For a party I make a bit more of an effort and there are recipes here for all occasions. I hope you enjoy them all.

People eat with their eyes, and I have to congratulate Aaron McLean on his eye for food photography. He has a wonderful ability for looking at a dish and knowing what bowl, plate or platter it should be on, what background and what accessories need to be in the shot to show it at its best. He also has a great understanding of the need to achieve a balance of images for a book to look just right. Working with Aaron has been a lot of fun.

the cook

israeli couscous, mango & pomegranate salad

serves 8 as a side dish

I believe this is one of the best salads I have ever made — it has so much flavour and texture. It is a meal in itself, however I sometimes serve it with grilled chicken thighs for a more substantial meal. Pomegranates are available in New Zealand supermarkets from around November through to March. I find it's hard to beat a good quality home-grown extra virgin olive oil to dress this simple salad.

200g Israeli couscous
1 mango
1 pomegranate
1 red capsicum
1 green capsicum
1 yellow capsicum
1 small red onion
2 cups cherry tomatoes
$\frac{1}{2}$ cup roughly chopped flat-leaf parsley
$\frac{1}{2}$ cup roughly chopped basil
$\frac{1}{2}$ cup pine nuts, toasted
extra virgin olive oil for dressing
salt and pepper

Cook the couscous according to packet instructions, drain and set aside to cool.

Separate the mango flesh from its seed. Peel and dice the flesh.

Cut the pomegranate in half and deseed over a sieve to retain the juice. Pick any pith out from the seeds.

Cut all the capsicums in half, remove the cores and seeds. Slice the flesh into thin strips.

Put all the ingredients in a large bowl, including the pomegranate juice, and toss lightly to combine. Drizzle with a little olive oil and season to taste.

salt brine for barbecued chicken

serves 4

I find that grilled chicken can be very dry. Curing the chicken in salt brine plumps it up and the meat is a lot more tender after cooking.

Some years ago I used to prepare smoked chipotle peppers this way for a real Tex-Mex flavour.

I recommend you buy a new plastic bucket and keep it just for this process. If you can't fit it into your fridge use a large bowl instead — just make sure all the chicken is covered with the brine.

If kosher salt is unavailable use rock salt.

4 litres water
½ cup sugar
1 cup kosher salt
¼ cup cardamom pods
¼ cup Szechwan peppercorns
1 tablespoon star anise
4 whole chicken legs, thighs attached

Put the water, sugar and salt in a large saucepan and bring to the boil. Stir to dissolve the sugar and salt. Add the spices, remove from the heat and set aside to cool. Transfer the brine to a large, clean bucket.

Prick the skin on the chicken legs with a fork and place into the cold salt brine. Weigh down if necessary to make sure all the chicken pieces are submerged. Refrigerate for at least 24 hours.

Cook on a preheated barbecue for 35 minutes or until the juices run clear, turning a few times to ensure even cooking.

Alternatively, slat-brined chicken pieces can be cooked in a conventional oven at 175°C but it will take a little longer — approximately 1 hour.

Variations
· For turkey, double the recipe and follow the above instructions.
· For pork loin, double the recipe, follow the above instructions but leave in the brine for 3–4 days.

spaghetti puttanesca

serves 4

'Sauce of whores' — need I say more? Yes, I must add that it tastes great and is simple to prepare.

1 tablespoon olive oil
2 cloves garlic, crushed
6 anchovy fillets (to taste)
⅓ cup dry white wine
1 x 400g tin whole peeled tomatoes, hand-crushed
2 tablespoons capers
⅓ cup kalamata olives
1 finely chopped red chilli (to taste, including seeds if you like it fiery)
250g dried Italian spaghetti
¼ cup coarsely chopped Italian flat-leaf parsley
freshly shaved Parmesan cheese for serving

Heat the olive oil in a frying pan over a low heat. Add the garlic and cook until golden. Add the anchovies and lightly fry with the garlic for 1–2 minutes. Add a splash of the wine to deglaze the pan. Add the tomatoes, the rest of the wine, capers, olives and chilli. Bring to a gentle simmer. Reduce heat and continue simmering for 20–25minutes until the sauce has reduced by about one third.

   Meanwhile, cook pasta according to packet instructions until al dente.

   To serve, add parsley to the sauce and stir through. Pour the sauce over the warm pasta and garnish with the grated Parmesan.

stuffed baked pumpkin with quinoa & prunes

serves 8

Amounts for this are only approximate — you will need to adjust them depending on the size of the pumpkin. I especially like the juiciness and flavour the prunes add to this dish.

The spice mix is more than you will need but you can store the rest in an airtight container until required — it's also delicious used as a rub for chicken.

1 cup quinoa (amount used will depend on the size of the pumpkin)
1 onion, finely diced
6 cloves garlic, diced
olive oil
1 red capsicum, deseeded and diced

1 courgette, diced
rind of 1 lemon
4 tablespoons spice mix (see below)
salt and pepper
1 cup pitted prunes, roughly chopped
1 x 2.5–3kg pumpkin, scrubbed

Cook the quinoa according to packet instructions. Drain and set aside until required.

Put the onion, garlic and a little olive oil in a frying pan and sauté until transparent. Add the capsicum, courgette, lemon rind and spice mix and sauté for 2–3 minutes. Season with salt and pepper. Remove from heat and fold through the quinoa and prunes.

Remove the crown from the pumpkin and set aside to use as a lid. Remove seeds and wipe the inside of the pumpkin with a paper towel. Push the filling into the pumpkin as tightly as possible. Spoon oil over the stuffing ensuring all the quinoa is covered. Put the crown on top and bake for 1–1¼ hours in oven preheated to 160°C until the pumpkin is tender.

spice mix
8 tablespoons coriander seeds
4 tablespoons cumin seeds

4 tablespoons fenugreek seeds

Dry roast the seeds for 20 minutes in an oven preheated to 160°C. Remove from the oven, cool and crush with a mortar and pestle to desired texture. Store in an airtight container until required.

greek-style baked cannellini beans with chicken balls

serves 4

This is the sort of dish I cook on Sunday nights during the winter. It can be prepared during the day and finished in the oven while you bath the kids or relax with a pre-dinner drink.

tomato sauce

1 onion, diced

4 cloves garlic, finely diced

olive oil

2 x 400g tins whole peeled tomatoes, hand-crushed

1 teaspoon dried wild oregano

1 cup dry white wine

2 bay leaves

salt and pepper

2 x 400g tins cannellini beans

350g feta, crumbled

Put the onion, garlic and a little olive oil in a preheated frying pan and sauté until transparent. Add the tomatoes and stir to combine. Add the oregano, wine and bay leaves and cook to reduce by about 50 per cent, stirring regularly — it needs to be thickened but not too wet. Season to taste, remove from the heat, remove the bay leaves and set aside until required.

To serve, rinse and drain the cannellini beans. Fold the drained beans through the tomato sauce. Pour the sauce into an ovenproof dish, place the chicken balls evenly on top and sprinkle the feta over. Bake in an oven preheated to 170°C for 30 minutes or until sauce is bubbling and feta has a golden finish. Serve piping hot with a loaf of sourdough.

chicken balls

500g lean chicken mince

²/₃ cup breadcrumbs

6 fresh sage leaves

1 teaspoon fresh thyme

2 tablespoons chopped mint

2 tablespoons chopped basil

2 fresh chillies, deseeded and finely diced (optional, according to taste)

flour for rolling

oil for frying

Put all the ingredients in a bowl and, using your hands, mix to combine. Shape into 24 small balls. Roll balls in a little flour then brown in a little oil in a frying pan preheated to a medium heat.

italian fish stew

serves 4

This is one of the most memorable meals I have ever eaten. I well remember the seaside restaurant in Positano, Italy. When Felix, our first born, was about 6 months old we decided to have a holiday. Taking a baby to Italy had advantages and disadvantages and I remember struggling to eat this wonderful stew with a wriggling baby in a front pack. One of the staff noticed my predicament and kindly offered to look after Felix while we ate our meal — bliss!

Cooking times for the dish will vary depending on the size of the fish.

200g mussels, scrubbed clean and
  beards removed
1½ cups dry white wine
200g other shellfish, scrubbed clean
10ml olive oil
2 onions, diced
1 bulb garlic, crushed and skins
  removed
1 teaspoon dried wild oregano
1 fresh chilli, deseeded and finely
  chopped (optional, according
  to taste)

2 x 400g tins whole peeled tomatoes,
  hand-crushed
1 whole baby snapper
600g firm, white-fleshed fish fillets
12 tiger prawns
⅓ cup chopped flat-leaf parsley
salt and pepper

Put the mussels in a large saucepan with 1 cup of the white wine and steam until they open. Remove the mussels and steam the other shellfish until cooked. Drain, reserving the liquid until required.

Return the pan to the heat and add the oil, onion and garlic and sauté until lightly browned. Add reserved liquid, remaining wine, oregano and chilli, if using, and the tomatoes. Cook over a gentle heat for 15 minutes.

Add the snapper and after 4 minutes turn it over and add the fillets. Move the fish around to ensure it all cooks evenly, taking care to avoid breaking it. After a couple of minutes add the prawns and the reserved shellfish and parsley. Gently heat through for a few minutes. Season with salt and pepper to taste.

Divide the whole fish evenly into 4 portions and place in 4 large serving bowls. Divide the rest of the stew evenly between the bowls and serve immediately with a crusty baguette.

snowpea, mushroom & pancetta risotto

serves 6

Risottos are really easy to make but are such a rewarding meal on a cold night. They are also endlessly adaptable. I came up with this version when I got home from work and discovered all we had in the fridge were mushrooms and snow peas. It was a real winner — the chewy texture of the mushrooms works well with the crunchiness and vibrancy of the blanched snow peas.

olive oil
2 shallots, peeled and finely diced
4 cloves garlic, finely diced
100g pancetta piece, cubed
2 cups arborio rice
1 cup dry white wine
500ml vegetable stock
1 cup shiitake mushrooms, sliced
1½ cups wood-ear mushrooms, torn into pieces
juice of 1 lemon
knob of butter
⅓ cup grated Parmesan cheese
a few sprigs of fresh thyme
2 large handfuls of snow peas, blanched and refreshed in iced water
salt and pepper

Heat a little olive oil in a heavy-based frying pan and sauté the shallots, garlic and pancetta until the shallots are transparent. Add the rice and stir to coat well. Add the wine and stir well to deglaze the pan. Add 1 cup of stock and the mushrooms and cook until the liquid has been absorbed. Keep adding the stock a ladleful at a time and continue cooking, stirring until all the liquid has been absorbed between each addition and the rice is al dente. Add the lemon juice, butter, Parmesan cheese, thyme and snow peas and fold through. Season with salt and pepper and serve immediately.

osso bucco

serves 4

There are many varieties of osso bucco, but this one is unusual in that it can be cooked on the stove top and its flavours are very simple. The intense herby flavour is enhanced by the wine and garlic. Other meats can be used but cooking times will vary depending upon the type of meat you use and the thickness of the cut.

4 venison shank pieces, cut into slices 2–3cm thick
plain flour for dusting
1 tablespoon olive oil
1 tablespoon butter
4 bay leaves
small bunch of fresh sage leaves
2 sprigs of rosemary
4 cloves garlic, finely diced
1 bottle of white wine (more or less)
salt and pepper

Coat the venison pieces with the flour. Heat the oil and butter in a large frying pan and brown the meat on all sides

Add bay leaves, sage, rosemary, garlic and $\frac{1}{2}$ cup of the white wine. Cover well and reduce temperature to a gentle simmer and cook for $1\frac{1}{2}$ hours or so, until meat is tender and coming away from the bone — you will need to keep an eye on it to make sure it doesn't dry out. Turn the pieces of meat occasionally to ensure even cooking and add more wine as required. After 1 hour of cooking, season with salt and pepper.

Remove meat from the pan and transfer to a dish and keep warm until required. Drain any excess fat from the pan and add extra wine to deglaze the pan.

Put the osso bucco onto serving plates and pour the pan juices over.

slow-roasted leg of lamb with olives & whisky

serves a crowd

Slowly roasting large pieces of meat helps to bring out the flavour — my mate Murray would cook a dish like this in his hooded barbecue for 5–6 hours for a really intense flavour. The whisky and olives make for a really rich dish.

Served with red cabbage and truffle-infused mashed potatoes (see overleaf) this is a knock-out dish for a special occasion.

olive oil

1 whole, bone-in leg of lamb
  (approximately 2.3kg)

1 large onion, diced

1 bulb garlic, peeled and crushed

200g kalamata olives, pitted

1 cup whisky

1 cup whole peeled tomatoes,
  hand-crushed

2 tablespoons chopped rosemary

2 tablespoons chopped thyme

salt and pepper

Brown the lamb on all sides — I prefer to do this in a little oil in a large casserole dish on the stove top. Alternatively, you can do this on a preheated barbecue hotplate.

Remove the lamb from the dish and add the onion and garlic and sauté until transparent. Add the browned lamb, half the whisky, tomatoes, rosemary, and thyme. Cover with a lid or tin foil and cook for 1 ½ hours in an oven preheated to 160°C turning 2–3 times during cooking to ensure it cooks evenly.

Add the olives and remaining whisky and replace the lid or cover. Cook for a further 30 minutes, remove the lid, turn the meat and cook for a further 30 minutes spooning the sauce over regularly.

Remove the meat from the pan and set aside for 15 minutes to rest before carving.

Meanwhile drain any excess fat from the liquid in the casserole dish. Place over a medium heat and cook, stirring continuously to reduce liquid to a nice sauce consistency. Pour over the lamb and serve immediately with red cabbage and mash (see page 124).

truffle-infused mash

serves 6–8

To honour the truffle, it is really important that the mashed potato is lump-free and velvety smooth.

250–300g potatoes, peeled
1 knob butter (1 tablespoon more or less to taste)
a decent splash of good olive oil (40ml more or less to taste)
2 tablespoons truffle oil or 1 teaspoon grated truffle (more or less to taste)
sea salt and freshly ground pepper

Put the potatoes into a large saucepan of boiling salted water and boil until tender when pricked with a knife. Drain well to avoid watery mash and return the potatoes to the saucepan. Add butter and olive oil and mash until smooth and velvety. Add the truffle oil or grated truffle and stir through. Season to taste with salt and pepper.

red cabbage with pear & balsamic

serves 6–8

This is best made in advance as it keeps in the refrigerator for a couple of days.

1 whole red cabbage, central stalk removed, very finely sliced
3 pears, peeled, cores removed, diced
2 cloves garlic, finely diced
2 tablespoons brown sugar
2 tablespoons balsamic vinegar
100g butter, melted

Place the cabbage, pears, garlic, brown sugar and vinegar in a large saucepan over a medium heat. Stir to combine. Add the butter and cook, stirring from time to time, for 1 hour or until the cabbage softens.

beef goulash

serves 4

This rustic dish, suitable for a cold winter's night, just needs a good crusty baguette and a glass of wine. Customers are often surprised when I tell them that I use blade steak for this dish — they are delighted to discover that such a rich casserole can be made with such a cheap cut of meat.

4–6 tablespoons olive oil
500g blade steak, cubed
flour for dusting
$\frac{1}{2}$ cup red wine
2 onions, diced
6 cloves garlic, crushed and finely chopped
2 tablespoons paprika
1 teaspoon cumin seeds, lightly toasted and crushed with a mortar and pestle
pinch of nutmeg
1 x 400g tin whole peeled tomatoes
2 green capsicums, deseeded and diced
1 leek, cleaned and sliced
1–1$\frac{1}{2}$ cups beef stock
salt and pepper
$\frac{1}{3}$ cup light sour cream
chopped fresh herbs for garnish (optional)

Heat half the oil in a large frying pan over a medium heat. Dust the meat in a little flour and brown in batches. Set aside. Use a splash of the wine to deglaze the pan. Add the rest of the oil, the onion, garlic, paprika, cumin seeds and nutmeg. Gently fry for 5 minutes, stirring frequently. Return the meat to the pan along with the tomatoes, capsicums and leek. Cook for 15 minutes, stirring occasionally.

Add the stock and remaining wine and season with salt and pepper. Cover and simmer over a low heat for 1–1$\frac{1}{2}$ hours until the meat is tender. Stir in the sour cream and sprinkle chopped herbs on top, if using.

roast poussin with juniper, orange & black pepper

serves 6

The juniper orange butter is fantastic, making this dish a sure crowd pleaser.
The recipe is just as good with chicken.

6 poussins
1 tablespoon juniper berries
1 tablespoon black peppercorns
250g butter, softened
2 cloves garlic, crushed and finely diced
juice of $\frac{1}{2}$ orange
a few sage leaves
20ml dry white wine
20ml chicken stock
salt and pepper

Wash the inside of the poussins and pat the cavities dry with paper towels.

Crush the juniper berries with a mortar and pestle. Transfer to a bowl and crush the black peppercorns the same way. Add to the juniper berries along with the butter, garlic and orange juice and mix to form a smooth paste. Smear the mixture over the poussins, making sure all the skin is covered. Place in a large pan or casserole that can go in the oven and can be used on the stove top. Roast for 25–30 minutes in a preheated oven set to 170°C or until cooked — the juices should run clear when a skewer is inserted into the bird between the breast and leg. Remove the poussins from the pan and set aside to rest until ready to serve.

Meanwhile deglaze the pan with the wine and stock and simmer to reduce and thicken the pan juices. Season to taste with salt and pepper.

To serve, place the poussins on a serving dish and pour the thickened sauce over.

hot as hell sauce

makes 3 cups

More of a salsa than a sauce, I like this for its heat and its spectacular colour and texture. I also love the yin and yang of the sweet pawpaw and the citric hit of fresh lime juice. I tried it out on Eric, one of my Thai chefs, and it was almost too hot for him — I suggest you wear disposable rubber gloves when handling the habañeros. Serve it with grilled fish or chicken or even as a dip.

1 red capsicum, deseeded and finely diced
2 tomatoes, deseeded and finely diced
1 pawpaw, deseeded, peeled and finely diced
2 spring onions, finely sliced
1–2 habañero chillies, deseeded and finely diced
1 teaspoon finely minced fresh ginger
2–3 tablespoons lime juice
1 teaspoon sea salt

Gently stir all the ingredients together until combined. Cover and refrigerate for at least 1 hour before serving.

roast turkey with pomegranate & vanilla sauce

serves 8–12

Try this next Christmas. It's a traditional Venetian dish prepared to celebrate the onset of spring and the pairing of pomegranate and vanilla is quite stunning.

roast turkey

1 small turkey (approximately 3kg — increase ingredients for a larger bird)
½ cup mint
2 tablespoons butter, softened
1–2 oranges, halved

extra butter for smearing on turkey skin
150ml extra virgin olive oil
salt and pepper

Clean turkey cavity and wipe inside and out with paper towels. Combine the mint and butter, add the oranges and place into the cavity. Tie up the legs and wings.

Place the turkey in a roasting dish and smear with butter. Pour oil over. Season with salt and pepper and place in a preheated oven set at 160°C. Roast for 2 ½ –3 hours, basting regularly, turning the bird a couple of times to ensure even cooking.

pomegranate & vanilla sauce

3 cups bottled pomegranate juice
2 pomegranates

seeds scraped from 1 vanilla pod
salt and pepper

Bring the pomegranate juice to the boil and simmer to reduce by one third. Deseed the pomegranates over a sieve, taking care to remove all pith. Retain the seeds and the juice and add to the saucepan along with the vanilla seeds. Heat and season to taste with salt and pepper.

smoked fish, green bean & potato salad with horseradish dressing

serves 4 as a main or 6 as a side dish

This is a good hearty salad. I have used smoked tuna because it flakes well but you can substitute other fish if you prefer.

salad
250g gourmet potatoes, peeled and cut in half
250g green beans
400g smoked tuna
1 cup cherry tomatoes

Cook the potatoes in boiling salted water until just tender. Drain and set aside to cool. Trim the beans, blanch and refresh in iced water.

Flake the fish, taking care to ensure all bones are removed and place in a bowl with the potatoes, beans and tomatoes. Pour the dressing over the salad and gently toss to combine.

dressing
2 tablespoons horseradish sauce (more or less to taste)
$\frac{1}{2}$ cup sour cream
juice of 1 lemon
2 tablespoons chopped mint
salt and pepper

Whisk all the ingredients together until combined. Season to taste with salt and pepper.

vietnamese lemongrass roasted ribs

serves 6

A really simple way to prepare ribs — the key to this is to cut the lemongrass as finely as possible.

1 ½–2kg pork ribs
2 stalks lemongrass, bashed and very finely chopped
6 cloves garlic, finely diced
2 teaspoons Chinese five spice powder
3 tablespoons fish sauce
a little oil

Put all the ingredients in a sturdy plastic bag and squish to ensure all the ribs are coated in the marinade. Refrigerate overnight then cook under a hot grill for 30–40 minutes, turning regularly, until cooked through.

classic steamed mussels

serves 4

This classic Kiwi mussel dish can be enjoyed anywhere any time. Some nights when I'm kaput from work I'll grab some mussels from my local fish shop on the way home. We all sit on the couch with a bowl on the floor that we throw the discarded shells into. All it needs is a good bread to soak up the leftover sauce.

olive oil
1 large onion, diced
1 cup white wine
6 cloves garlic, roughly diced
1 ½ –2kg mussels, scrubbed and beards removed
⅓ cup chopped Italian flat-leaf parsley
freshly cracked pepper

Heat a little oil in a large saucepan over medium heat. Add the onion and cook until transparent. Add the wine, garlic and mussels. Cover and bring to the boil. Reduce the heat and steam the mussels for 4–5 minutes until they have all opened. Stir a few times to ensure they are all cooked — discard any that have not opened. Add the parsley and cracked pepper, stir and serve in large bowls with the sauce spooned over.

green prawn curry

serves 6

This is an amazingly simple curry to make. I have used prawns but any seafood can be substituted. When I have made it at Zarbo the chefs have actually stolen some of the paste and used it to smear on the baked salmon — it's that good.

2 red onions, finely chopped
6 cloves garlic, finely chopped
2.5cm piece ginger, peeled and finely chopped
2 bunches of coriander, roots and stalks, cleaned and roughly chopped
grapeseed oil
750g prawns, cleaned and deveined
1 teaspoon cardamom pods
1 teaspoon turmeric powder
1 teaspoon cumin seeds, toasted and ground with a mortar and pestle
2 red chillies, finely chopped (according to taste)
6–8 teaspoons unsweetened yoghurt
1 cup coconut milk
fresh coriander for garnish

Put the onion, garlic, ginger and coriander in a food processor and blend to form a smooth paste — add a little water if necessary and set aside until required.

Heat 1 tablespoon of oil in a large frying pan or wok, add the prawns and cook until just coloured on both sides — you will need to do this in batches to stop the wok losing heat. Set aside the cooked prawns until required.

Wipe out the pan or wok and add 1 tablespoon of oil. Return it to the heat and add cardamom, turmeric and cumin and stir to combine. Add the onion paste and stir over a medium heat for a few minutes. Add the chilli and season with salt. Reduce the heat right down and add the yoghurt 1 teaspoon at a time, stirring constantly to make sure that the sauce does not split.

Add the prawns and coconut milk and simmer for a few more minutes until the prawns are cooked through. Serve with rice and garnish with chopped coriander.

kumara & pumpkin salad with pear maple syrup & yoghurt

serves 6–8

It is not often that I specify a store-bought dressing in a recipe — unless it is from my Zarbo range — but this Fresh Fields brand pear and maple syrup is a fantastic new product from ENZA that deserves a place in your pantry. Here, the unsweetened yoghurt cuts through the sweetness of the syrup. The syrup is also great with ice cream for dessert or pancakes for breakfast.

700g kumara, peeled and diced
700g pumpkin, peeled and diced
grapeseed oil
2 handfuls of rocket
$\frac{1}{2}$ cup pumpkin seeds, toasted
salt and pepper
$\frac{1}{2}$ cup pear maple syrup
$\frac{1}{2}$ cup unsweetened yoghurt

Cook the kumara in a saucepan of boiling salted water until just tender. Drain well and set aside to cool. Put the pumpkin in a roasting dish and add a little oil. Using your hands, toss the pumpkin in the oil to ensure it is well coated and place in the oven preheated to 180°C. Bake for 15–20 minutes until just cooked. Remove from the oven and set aside to cool.

To serve, put the kumara, pumpkin, rocket and pumpkin seeds in a bowl and toss lightly together. Pour on the pear maple syrup and toss through the salad. Arrange on a platter and spoon the yoghurt over the top.

beetroot, grilled lamb & haloumi salad

serves 6–8

A nice colourful salad with great flavours — you can either boil the beetroot or roast it in the oven for a more intense flavour as I have here.

salad

1.5kg beetroot, peeled and diced
olive oil
2 teaspoons dried mint
350g lamb loin

250g haloumi, finely sliced
2 handfuls of rocket
1 red onion, sliced into rings
salt and pepper

dressing

60ml raspberry vinegar
30ml sherry vinegar

40ml olive oil
2 cloves garlic, diced

Put the beetroot in a roasting dish and add a little oil. Using your hands, toss the beetroot in the oil to ensure it is well coated and place in the oven preheated to 180°C. Bake for 15–20 minutes until just cooked. Remove from the oven and set aside to cool.

Meanwhile, rub a little oil and the dried mint into the lamb and cook on a preheated grill plate for 3–4 minutes on each side until cooked through. It should still be pink in the centre. Set aside to cool.

Sear the haloumi slices on both sides in a preheated grill pan.

Whisk all the dressing ingredients together until combined.

To serve, put all the ingredients in a bowl and add the dressing. Toss gently to combine. Season to taste with salt and pepper.

root vegetable salad platter

serves 6–8 as a side dish

Farmers' markets are becoming increasingly popular and I really enjoy a stroll around my local — Parnell Farmers' Market. I go there regularly to stock up on fresh, seasonal vegetables. When making this platter, I like to leave some of the stalks on the root vegetables to give the dish a truly rustic appearance. It can look dramatic with just a couple of vegetables; for example carrot and parsnip, or with a number of the season's offerings as shown here.

The dressing is one of the store-cupboard basics that I keep in the fridge at home.

2.5kg mixed root vegetables

dressing
2 cloves garlic, finely diced
½ cup olive oil
60ml balsamic vinegar
2 tablespoons chopped fresh mint
salt and pepper

Blanch the vegetables and refresh in iced water. Drain well and set aside until required.

Whisk all the dressing ingredients together until combined.

To serve, arrange the vegetables on a platter and add the dressing. Toss gently to combine.

udon noodles with seasonal vegetables & spicy peanut dressing

serves 4

You can use any seasonal vegetables to make this reliable, comforting, quick-and-easy meal all year round.

noodles

400g udon noodles

1 bunch asparagus, trimmed

1 head broccoli, cut into
    bite-sized florets

1 red capsicum, deseeded
    and finely sliced

1 cup snow peas

2/3 cup coriander, chopped

1cm piece ginger, peeled
    and julienned

Cook the noodles according to packet instructions. Blanch the asparagus and broccoli in boiling water and refresh in iced water. Drain well. Put the vegetables, snow peas, coriander, ginger and noodles in a bowl, pour on the dressing and toss gently together. Arrange on a platter or in individual bowls and serve immediately.

spicy peanut dressing

makes 2 cups

This is another favourite of mine to have ready in the fridge for those nights when it all seems too much!

1/2 cup chunky peanut butter

3/4–1 cup water

2 cloves garlic, crushed

2 teaspoons grated ginger

1 small red chilli, deseeded and
    finely chopped

80ml light soy sauce

80ml sesame oil

a dash of fish sauce

60ml sweetened rice vinegar

Blend the peanut butter and 3/4 cup water together in a small saucepan. Add extra water if necessary to form a smooth but runny paste. Add remaining ingredients and, stirring continuously, bring to the boil. Reduce heat and, continuing to stir, simmer gently for 5 minutes.

summer pasta salad

serves 4

This is a classic deli-style salad. With a dish like this most flavour combinations will work. I'm not big on creamy dressings — hence the very simple olive oil and lemon juice here, but feel free to please yourself.

salad
250g dried pasta
1 bunch asparagus, chargrilled
$\frac{1}{4}$ pumpkin, deseeded, peeled, diced and roasted
1 cup kalamata olives
1 cup semi-dried tomatoes
1 x 400g tin chargrilled artichokes, drained and cut in half

dressing
juice of 2 lemons
125ml olive oil
$\frac{2}{3}$ cup chopped fresh mint
salt and pepper

Cook the pasta according to packet instructions.

Combine the pasta, asparagus, pumpkin, olives, tomatoes and artichokes in a large bowl.

To make the dressing, put the lemon juice into a bowl and slowly whisk in the olive oil. Add the mint and season with salt and pepper. Stir to combine. Pour dressing over the salad and gently toss to combine.

desserts

desserts

What are desserts? Are they designed to finish off a great meal, the luxury of something sweet and sensual, or do they make up for a bad main course? Whatever way you spin it, desserts are usually some sort of bakery-related product dressed up with things that complement, enhance, highlight, balance or embellish it. This leads to the next question. What is the difference between a pudding and a dessert? I think of puddings as homely and rustic and usually cooked. (And, just to confuse things, there are savoury puddings too – Yorkshire pudding served with roast beef in a traditional Sunday lunch, black pudding or a winter-warming steak and kidney pudding.) Traditionally, desserts were uncooked and made with fresh fruit. Nowadays they are often lighter and more sophisticated concoctions – think chocolate mousse, refreshing champagne jelly and lighter-than-air soufflé. Desserts are all about structure, texture, flavour and elegant presentation.

I have included a few classic desserts of restaurant standard so you can understand that creating exciting desserts is not that complicated — it's about planning ahead and being organised. I have added some twists to turn the ordinary into the extraordinary!

When creating a dessert that has elements of structure, height, texture and also accompanying bits and pieces, I always start off with an A4 sheet of paper and a pencil, and do a little sketch of the finished product. I want to see how my dessert will look on paper before I go to all the trouble of making all the components and then find out that it just does not work. The colours may be wrong or the plate may not be big enough to take all the elements of the dessert. Any good pastry chef, baker or chef will do this basic task. You don't have to be an artist, but you do need to understand a little bit about symmetry, balance, design and colours.

So, pudding or dessert? In the end it doesn't really matter. Both appear on menus in country pubs, cafés, and fine dining establishments. Both are served as the final act, the encore to a meal – either one should be a beautifully presented dish that leaves your guests speechless.

the baker

sour cherry & cranberry trifle

serves 4

What would Christmas be without trifle? The layers and angles of this one and the sharp cherry flavour combined with the creamy sweetness of the custard will make it the highlight of your next Christmas get-together. You can make your own sponge (see page 227) or use store-bought sponge fingers. The key to this dessert is co-ordinating the jelly and custard to make sure they are ready when you need them.

cranberry jelly
2 sheets leaf gelatine
300ml cranberry juice
50g sugar

Soak the gelatine in cold water to soften. Bring the cranberry juice and sugar almost to the boil, remove from the heat. Squeeze excess water from the gelatine leaves and put them in the hot liquid. Stir until gelatine has dissolved. Pour into a jug and set aside to cool until required, but use before it sets.

custard

250ml milk	2 egg yolks
75ml single cream	15g sugar
1 vanilla pod, split and seeds scraped	1 teaspoon cornflour or corn starch

Bring the milk, cream and vanilla pod to simmering point over a low heat. Remove the vanilla pod — you can wash the vanilla pod, dry it and put it in a jar with caster sugar to make vanilla sugar.

Whisk the yolks, sugar and cornflour or corn starch together until well blended. Whisking continuously, pour the hot milk and cream into the eggs and sugar. Stirring gently over a low heat with a wooden spatula, continue cooking until the mixture has thickened — it should coat the back of the spoon. Pour the custard into a jug and cover with plastic wrap, cool a little, and then use while still pouring consistency.

sour cherry filling

1 x 425g tin pitted sour cherries	1 tablespoon cornflour or
1 vanilla pod, cut lengthways	corn starch

Drain the juice from the cherries and set them aside until required. Pour 150ml of the cherry juice into a small saucepan and scrape the seeds from the vanilla pod into the juice and add the pod, too. Mix the cornflour with 1 tablespoon of the cherry juice to make a slurry. Set aside. Bring the juice to the boil and remove from the heat. Whisk in the cornflour or corn starch slurry. Stirring constantly, return the saucepan to a medium heat and cook for 2 minutes or until thickened. Remove from the heat and stir in the cherries — it's okay if a few of the cherries break up, as this will create texture. Pour the filling in to a bowl, cover with plastic wrap and set aside to cool until required.

100–150g sponge cake cut into 1cm cubes, or
   sponge fingers cut into pieces
1 batch crème chantilly (see page 242)
4 fresh strawberries for garnish

To assemble the trifles, arrange 4 x 250ml glasses in a bowl or box at an angle of 45°, making sure they are well supported and cannot tip over. Put 5–6 pieces of sponge or sponge finger in the bottom corner of each glass and pour in one-quarter of the cooled liquid jelly. Carefully transfer to the refrigerator until the jelly is set.

    To serve, remove glasses from the refrigerator and stand the glasses upright. Spoon a quarter of the custard into each glass then a quarter of the cherry filling. Finish with a dollop of crème chantilly and level the top. Decorate with a fresh strawberry.

rosé jelly with summer berries

serves 4

Rosé and summer fresh berries are simply elegant. You can use champagne or any good quality sparkling wine if you prefer, but I like the gorgeous colour the rosé adds. You'll need to keep these beauties chilled until 20 minutes before serving. Serve with tuiles (see page 161) or other dry petits fours (see pages 203, 205 and 207), as desired.

8 gelatine leaves
750ml rosé wine
500g caster sugar
6 small strawberries, hulled and
   cut into quarters

200g fresh raspberries
200g fresh blueberries
1 small peach, cut into thin slices

Soak the gelatine in cold water to soften. Bring the wine and sugar almost to the boil. Remove from the heat. Squeeze excess water from the gelatine leaves and put them in the hot liquid. Stir until the gelatine has dissolved. Pour into a jug and set aside to cool until lukewarm.

Pour 1cm of jelly into 4 x 250ml glasses and refrigerate until almost set.

Remove from the refrigerator and arrange some berries and peaches evenly over the layer of set jelly in each glass and carefully pour over another 1cm of liquid jelly. Return to the refrigerator until almost set. Repeat this process until all the berries, peach and jelly have been used. Place in the refrigerator overnight to set the jelly.

Place each glass on a white serving plate with two tuile biscuits or similar on the side.

plum & fennel tarte tatin with vanilla ice cream, calvados apple purée & white chocolate tuiles

serves 4

This classic dessert is a caramelised fresh fruit tart, baked upside down then turned out the right way again. You can use aniseed instead of fennel if you prefer. Serve this with your home-made vanilla ice cream (see page 245) and calvados apple purée (see page 242).

tarte

1 batch butter puff pastry
   (see page 224), chilled
5 Red Doris plums
100g unsalted butter, softened

220g caster sugar
¾ tablespoon fennel seeds, lightly
   bruised with a mortar and pestle

Remove the pastry from the refrigerator and allow to rest for 20 minutes at room temperature. Roll out on a lightly floured surface to 4–5mm thick. Cut out 4 x 12cm round circles. Wrap pastry scraps in plastic wrap and return to refrigerator for later.

Cut each plum in quarters and remove the stones.

Mix the butter, sugar and fennel seeds together to combine. Cook over a slow heat to melt the butter and dissolve the sugar mixture. Shake the pan gently to ensure even cooking and when the syrup is simmering evenly, turn the heat up and cook until thickened and golden brown, still gently shaking the pan occasionally. Pour the caramel mixture evenly into 4 small 10cm round pie dishes so there is a 5mm layer of caramel in the bottom.

Arrange 5 plum quarters in a circle, skin-side down in each tin. Place a pastry circle on top of the plums, tucking the edges of the pastry inside the edge of the tins. Prick with a fork or knife several times to allow the steam to escape and prevent the pastry from doming. Bake for 10 minutes in a preheated oven set at 220°C then reduce the heat to 200°C and bake for a further 10–12 minutes until the pastry is golden brown and cooked through. Carefully remove the baked tartes from the oven and leave to cool for 3–4 minutes.

When still warm, carefully tip each tarte onto a serving plate — the caramelised plums will now be on top. Take extreme care when doing this, as the caramel syrup will still be runny and very hot.

Serve warm, with a scoop of vanilla ice cream topped with a white chocolate tuile on one side of each plate and a spoonful of calvados apple purée on the other.

white chocolate tuile
100g white chocolate

Melt the white chocolate in a bowl over a saucepan of simmering water.

While the chocolate is melting, cut 4 strips of acetate or non-stick baking paper each 1.5cm wide x 10cm long.

Using a palette knife, spread one side of each strip of paper with white chocolate and place onto a tray lined with non-stick baking paper. Put in the refrigerator to set. When ready to use, carefully peel off the acetate and use or store in a cool, dark place until required.

chocolate & blue cheese tortellini nestled on a bed of praline with caramel sauce

serves 4

The combination of chocolate and blue cheese makes this dessert unique — the sweetness of the praline and caramel sauce balances the blue cheese perfectly. If you can't get your head around the idea of blue cheese for pudding you can use a fresh or frozen raspberry inside the chocolate tortellini wrappers instead — but that should only be as a last resort!

filling

75ml cream

150g dark chocolate, chopped into
   small pieces

1 tablespoon unsalted butter

Heat the cream to just below boiling point. Add the chocolate and butter and stir until melted and combined. Cover and cool for 2 hours to set.

tortellini wrappers

15g cocoa powder

2 tablespoons hot water

2 tablespoons dark chocolate, melted

2 eggs

200g plain flour

50g sugar

Mix the cocoa and hot water together to make a paste. Mix the cocoa paste with the remaining ingredients to form a dough mass. Tip the dough out onto a lightly floured surface and knead for 10–15 minutes until the dough is smooth and elastic in feel. Take a rest period of 30 seconds every 2–3 minutes. Form into a ball, cover with plastic and place in the refrigerator for 1 hour to firm up a little.

On a lightly floured bench, roll out the dough into a 2–3mm thick rectangle. Cut into 12 x 7.5cm squares.

1 egg for egg wash

1 tablespoon water for egg wash

100g blue cheese

Whisk the egg and water together to make an egg wash.

Place 1 teaspoon of chocolate filling in the centre of each square and about $\frac{1}{2}$ teaspoon of blue cheese on top of the filling. Brush the edges with egg wash, fold over the squares to form triangles and pinch the edges to seal. Pull the 2 points on the long side of each triangle together and pinch firmly to form a tortellini shape. These can be made up to 2 days in advance, covered and kept in the refrigerator until required.

To serve, cook the tortellini for 3 minutes in gently simmering water until they float. Place a small amount of praline (see page 243) in the middle of 4 serving plates and top with a scoop of vanilla ice cream (see page 245). Drain the tortellini thoroughly and place 3 on the outside of each plate and drizzle some caramel sauce (see page 242) around the tortellini and ice cream. Serve immediately while the tortellini are still warm.

espresso crème brûlée with nougatine spoon

serves 4

With each spoonful this brûlée gives you the feeling you are having a latte at your favourite café in Paris. There are several layers of sophistication to this dessert — creamy smooth custard, satisfying coffee and the crunch of the toffee topping. The nougatine spoon is for fun to nibble on after the brûlée has gone. If you don't have an espresso machine you'll need to buy a double-shot espresso from your favourite cafe.

espresso brûlée

350ml fresh cream

150ml whole milk

50ml double espresso coffee

1 tablespoon Kahlùa

6 egg yolks from large eggs

25g sugar

4 tablespoons coffee crystal
    sugar for decoration

Heat the cream and milk in a heavy-based saucepan to just below boiling point. Remove from the heat, stir in the espresso and Kahlùa and set aside.

Whisk the egg yolks and sugar until pale and creamy in colour. Whisking well after each addition, pour the hot coffee cream mixture into the egg yolks and sugar. Strain the liquid through a very fine sieve and pour into 4 x 150ml coffee cups lightly greased with butter. Stand them on a baking tray and bake for 60–70 minutes in a preheated oven set at 150°C until set on top. To test if the custard is baked correctly, it should come away from the side of the cup when tilted but the centre should still remain a little wobbly. Alternatively, insert a sharp knife into the custard and it should come out almost clean. The custard will continue to cook for a few minutes after it comes out of the oven. Remove from the oven, and allow to cool at room temperature. Store in the refrigerator until required.

Remove cups from the refrigerator 30 minutes before serving to allow them to warm up a little. Sprinkle approximately 1 tablespoon of coffee crystals in a thin, even layer over the top of each custard cup. Using a gas blow torch, caramelise the sugar until a golden caramel syrup forms. Allow to harden. Place a nougatine spoon (see below) on the top of each coffee cup and serve on a saucer.

nougatine spoons

100g sugar

squeeze of lemon juice

75g flaked almonds, lightly toasted

Place the sugar and lemon juice into a heavy-based frying pan over a medium heat. Stir constantly until a golden caramel syrup forms. Add the toasted almond flakes. Tip onto a lightly oiled bench and roll to 2–3mm thick. Quickly cut teaspoon shapes from the toffee and while it is still hot, mould the pieces over large teaspoons. You must work quickly to make these spoons before the toffee hardens. If, however, the toffee does set you can place it on a baking tray lined with non-stick baking paper in a warm oven to soften. Store in an airtight container until required.

lemon cream mille-feuille with strawberry & raspberry compote, aged balsamic reduction, basil syrup & gin jelly cubes

serves 4

There's a delicate balance of sharp flavours — aged balsamic reduction (see page 242), basil syrup (see page 242), and gin jelly cubes (see page 243) — at work here. It's not as hard to make as you might think — everything can be made the day before and assembled just before serving. It's child's play, really, much like building with blocks.

mille-feuille
12 x 4cm x 10cm x 3mm rectangles butter puff pastry (see page 224)

icing sugar for dusting

lemon cream filling
300g semi-whipped cream

1x full quantity of lemon curd (see page 243)

strawberry and raspberry compote
400g firm whole strawberries, hulled and cut into small cubes

150g raspberry coulis (see page 244)

Put the pastry rectangles on a baking tray lined with non-stick baking paper, sprinkle lightly with icing sugar and cover with non-stick baking paper. Place a baking tray on top and bake in a preheated oven set at 220°C until glazed and golden brown. Remove from the oven and transfer to a cooling rack until required.

To make the lemon cream, fold the cream and lemon curd together and whisk until firm. Cover and put in the refrigerator until required.

To make the compote, gently mix the strawberries and coulis together. Cover and put in the refrigerator until required.

To assemble the mille-feuille, put the lemon cream in a piping bag and pipe a small amount onto 4 of the cooled pastry rectangles. Repeat until you have 4 servings with 3 layers of pastry and 2 layers of cream. Dust the top of each mille-feuille with icing sugar and place on a serving plate. Arrange some gin jelly cubes alongside. Using 2 separate squirty bottles, decorate with a drizzle of basil syrup and a drizzle of balsamic reduction. Finish with some berry compote.

almond & walnut tartlets with toffee sauce & chocolate chip ice cream

serves 4

Walnut tarts are a feature of everyday life in some regions of France, but this is an indulgent dessert. You can serve it at room temperature or heat the tart in an oven set at 180°C for 10 minutes to serve warm. Serve it with toffee sauce (see page 244) and chocolate chip ice cream (see page 245).

almond cream filling

50g softened butter
50g sugar
1 egg, slightly warmed, lightly beaten
50g ground almonds

10g plain flour or strong
  bread flour
1 tablespoon walnut liqueur
  (optional)

1 batch sweet pastry (see page 224)

caramelised walnut topping

75ml fresh cream
120g sugar

110g walnut pieces, roughly chopped

To make the filling, use a wooden spoon to beat the butter and sugar together until light and creamy. Add the egg bit by bit, beating well after each addition to avoid curdling. Add the ground almonds, flour and walnut liqueur, if using, and mix well to form a smooth cream-like consistency. Set aside until required.

On a lightly floured work surface, roll out the sweet pastry to 3mm thick. Cut out circles to line the base and sides of 4 x 10cm round tarts tins. Trim off the top edges with a sharp knife.

Place a small amount of almond cream in the bottom of each pastry shell so that each is quarter full. Bake for 15 minutes in a preheated oven set at 200°C or until slightly golden brown in colour. Remove from the oven and cool in the tins.

While the tartlets are cooling, make the caramelised topping by heating the cream to just below boiling point. At the same time, caramelise the sugar, without adding any water, in a heavy-based saucepan on a medium heat.

As soon as the sugar reaches an amber colour, immediately remove the saucepan from the heat. Stirring constantly, gradually add the hot cream. Continue stirring to achieve a smooth creamy caramel then add the walnuts.

Immediately, fill the tart shells with the walnut topping, taking care to not over-fill the tarts. Set aside until required.

To serve, drizzle a circle of toffee sauce onto 4 serving plates and place the tartlets on top. Place a scoop of chocolate chip ice cream on the top of each tart and serve immediately.

sunken chocolate cake with vanilla honey-infused mascarpone & raspberry coulis

serves 10

I am not often a fan of chocolate but I love this recipe — the texture is somewhere between a chocolate mousse cake and a full-bodied chocolate cake. It works nicely with the raspberry coulis and vanilla and manuka honey mascarpone. The message in this dessert is keep it simple.

cake

225g good-quality dark chocolate
225g butter
60g plain flour
50g ground almonds
6 medium eggs, at room temperature
50g light soft brown sugar

175g caster sugar
melted butter and flour for
    coating the cake tin
cocoa powder for dusting
icing sugar for dusting

mascarpone

250g mascarpone
1 tablespoon manuka honey

seeds scraped from 1 vanilla pod

Put the chocolate and butter in a bowl over a saucepan of boiling water. Turn off the heat and allow the chocolate and butter to melt, stirring occasionally. Sift the flour and almonds together and stir into the melted chocolate mixture.

Whisk the eggs and sugars together until stiff and firm. Very gently fold the chocolate and egg mixtures together until just combined. Pour into a 20cm loose-bottomed cake tin that has been greased with butter and lightly coated with flour. Bake for 60–70 minutes in a preheated oven set at 170°C. Insert a skewer into the middle and if it comes out clean, the cake is ready. Transfer to a cooling rack. When completely cool, cut into 10 or 12 pieces and dust with cocoa powder and icing sugar.

Stir the mascarpone, honey and vanilla seeds together in a bowl to combine. Cover and put in the refrigerator until required.

To serve, place a portion of cake in the middle of a large white plate. Using a dessertspoon dipped into warm water, scoop some mascarpone onto one side and then spoon some raspberry coulis (see page 244) beside it, or place the coulis in a small pouring jug to one side.

cakes, cookies,
pastries &
petits fours

cakes, cookies, pastries & petits fours

Take one pound of sugar, one pound of butter, one pound of eggs and one pound of flour and you have all you need to make a traditional pound cake. The same four basic ingredients form the basis of most baking with the addition of a few fillings and flavourings. Understanding and mastering the basics makes baking an exciting challenge.

Ever since I can remember, my grandmother always had her cake tins filled with yummy banana loaves, gingerbread and madeira cakes — it's no surprise I have a sweet tooth with a preference for good, honest, rustic, home-baked cakes. What could be more satisfying than a really moist, luxurious carrot cake with a fluffy lemon-infused cream cheese icing?

The thing I like about being from a young country like New Zealand is the innovation shown in our home baking and also in our café scene. I often look to home for new ideas to flavour cakes, muffins and slices — I include slices in the cake category as many slices are formed by baking a cake in a shallow tin.

Another staple for many people is a good cookie to dunk into a consoling cup of coffee or tea. I love a simple butter shortbread made, once again, with four basic ingredients — icing sugar, butter, flour and cornflour. Cookies also form the basis of many other products; for example, as a crumb base for cheesecake; and the many variations of no-bake slices. The uncooked dough can also be used as a base for slices.

Pastry-making takes a bit of patience and practice, but it is well worth the effort as a good pastry will get you places. Sweet pastry can be endlessly adapted with nuts, cocoa powder, orange or lemon zest and, my personal favourite, vanilla. Short pastry combines flour, butter, salt and a little water to give a buttery, rich, crunchy finish that can't be beaten in quiches and meat pies. Sometimes I even use it as a base for sweet tarts to balance a particularly sweet filling. Puff pastry is the most difficult pastry to make — it's no wonder many home-bakers choose to buy ready-made puff pastry, but the down-side is that most ready-made products contain specialty margarine instead of butter and there is a marked difference in quality.

This is a collection of basic recipes with a few twists that make them fresh and modern. I hope you enjoy them all.

the baker

white chocolate chunk & cranberry chewy cookies

makes 20–22 large or 40 smaller cookies

White chocolate and cranberry are great partners — the sweetness of the chocolate and the tang of the cranberry balance each other perfectly. I like these chewy, but if you prefer crunchy cookies you can bake them a little bit longer than the recipe suggests.

135g butter, softened
100g sugar
100g soft, dark-brown sugar
1 small egg
10ml milk
a few drops of vanilla essence
150g plain flour
$\frac{1}{2}$ teaspoon baking soda
$\frac{1}{4}$ teaspoon baking powder

$\frac{1}{4}$ teaspoon salt
70g medium-sized rolled oats
100g dried cranberries, coarsely chopped
140g white chocolate drops, coarsely chopped

100g rolled jumbo oats for sprinkling

Put the butter and sugars in the bowl of an electric mixer fitted with a beater attachment and mix until light in colour, but not creamy and fluffy in texture. Add the egg, milk and vanilla essence and continue beating.

Sift the flour, baking soda, baking powder and salt together and add to the creamed mixture along with the rolled oats. Mix until well combined. Add the cranberries and white chocolate and mix again until evenly distributed.

Using a tablespoon and floured hands, scoop spoonfuls of dough — 35g each — and roll into balls. Place balls 10cm apart on baking trays lined with non-stick baking paper and sprinkle with extra rolled oats. Don't flatten the balls or the cookies will spread too much.

Bake in a preheated oven set at 170–175°C for 10–12 minutes until golden brown. Remove from the oven and transfer to a cooling rack.

gingernut-style cookies

makes about 16–18

When Toni Causley, winner of 'Nestlé New Zealand's Hottest Home Baker' TV show, made these for me to judge I felt the need for a good cup of Earl Grey tea to get dunking. They are so good I wanted to include them here and Toni kindly agreed. Toni also crushed these cookies to make a cheesecake base.

250g plain flour
2 teaspoons ground ginger
2 teaspoons baking soda
$^3/_4$ teaspoon ground cardamom
$^3/_4$ teaspoon ground cinnamon
$^1/_2$ teaspoon ground coriander
$^1/_4$ teaspoon freshly ground black pepper
$^1/_4$ teaspoon salt
100g chopped crystallised ginger
170g soft brown sugar
125g butter, softened
70g vegetable shortening, softened
1 large egg
90g honey

1 cup raw sugar for rolling

Sift the flour, ground ginger, baking soda, cardamom, cinnamon, coriander, pepper and salt together into a medium-sized bowl. Add the ginger and set aside until required. Put the brown sugar, butter and shortening in the bowl of an electric mixer fitted with a beater attachment and beat until creamy but not fluffy. Add the egg and honey and beat until blended. Stir in the flour mixture, mixing until just blended. Cover and refrigerate for 1 hour.

Spread the raw sugar on a flat plate. Remove the cookie dough from the refrigerator. Using a tablespoon, scoop large spoonfuls of dough — approximately 50g each — and, using wet hands, roll into balls. Roll the balls in raw sugar making sure they are completely coated. Place balls 5cm apart on baking trays that have been lightly sprayed with non-stick cooking spray and covered with non-stick baking paper.

Bake in an oven preheated to 170°C for 15–17 minutes until cracked on top but still soft to touch. Remove from the oven and cool on the baking trays for 5 minutes before carefully transferring to a cooling rack.

cranberry shortbread

makes about 25 pieces

Shortbread is a classic but sometimes even a classic needs a kick with cranberries. Cranberries are under-rated as a dried fruit. Sure they are a little sharp in taste but they are a lovely deep red. Phillippa Grogan from Phillippa's in Melbourne makes a similar shortbread which is very popular.

300g softened butter
170g sugar
400g standard plain flour
20g cornflour
40g rice flour
2 good pinches of salt
100g dried cranberries

caster sugar for dredging

Put the butter and sugar in the bowl of an electric mixer fitted with a beater attachment and beat until light and fluffy. Sift the flour, cornflour, rice flour and salt together. Add half the dry ingredients to the creamed butter and sugar and beat again until light. On slow speed, blend in the remaining dry ingredients until the dough comes away from the sides of the mixing bowl. Add the cranberries and continue to mix to form a dough mass.

Turn the dough onto a lightly floured bench and roll out to $1\frac{1}{2}$ cm thick. Cut into shapes with a shaped cutter or cut into squares, rectangles or triangles.

Put the shortbread on a baking tray lined with a double thickness of non-stick baking paper. Prick with a fork if desired. Bake in a preheated oven set at 180°C for 10–20 minutes until a very pale golden colour — time will depend on the size of the shapes. Remove from the oven and transfer to a cooling rack. Immediately dredge with caster sugar.

triple chocolate chunk & pecan cookies

makes 25

Karen Brown, a contestant in 'Nestlé New Zealand's Hottest Home Baker', made delicious Triple Chocolate Chunk Cookies but I wanted some nuttines so added pecans to the mix.

225g butter, softened
225g sugar
85g brown sugar
1 egg
1 egg white
2 teaspoons vanilla extract
250g standard flour
1 teaspoon baking powder
5g salt
115g white chocolate pieces, chopped into $\frac{1}{2}$ cm chunks
115g milk chocolate pieces, chopped into $\frac{1}{2}$ cm chunks
115g dark chocolate pieces, chopped into $\frac{1}{2}$ cm chunks
130g pecans, roughly chopped

Put the butter and two sugars in the bowl of an electric mixer fitted with a beater attachment and beat until pale, but not creamy and fluffy. Add the egg, egg white and vanilla and beat until combined.

Sift the flour, baking powder and salt together in a large mixing bowl and add half to the creamed mixture. Beat on low speed for 1 minute. Add the remaining dry ingredients and mix until almost all the flour is mixed in. Add the chocolate pieces and pecans and continue to mix until they are well combined.

Using a tablespoon, scoop large spoonfuls of dough — 50g each — and, using floured hands, roll into balls. Place balls 6cm apart on baking trays lined with non-stick baking paper.

Bake in an oven preheated to 175–180°C for 12–15 minutes until golden but still soft to touch. Remove from the oven and cool on the baking trays for 5 minutes before carefully transferring to a cooling rack. Don't be alarmed when they sink a little.

danish dream cake

makes 1x20cm cake

In Denmark they serve this delicious moist spongy coffee cake for afternoon tea. It's not a coffee cake because it contains coffee, but because you eat it with coffee in the afternoon. As the English have afternoon tea, the Danes have afternoon coffee. This cake is divine — I love the caramel flavour both in the cake and the topping. It can also be baked in a square or a rectangular cake tin.

cake
250g standard flour
3 teaspoons baking powder
50g butter, melted
200ml milk

4 eggs
300g brown sugar
1 teaspoon vanilla extract

topping
125g butter, softened
50ml milk
200g brown sugar

100g thread coconut, rubbed
    between your hands to break
    the strands up a little

Sift the flour and the baking powder into a large bowl. Whisk the butter and milk together. Put the eggs, sugar and vanilla in the bowl of an electric mixer fitted with a whisk and beat until light and fluffy. Fold in the flour, then fold in the butter and milk mixture.

Pour the batter into a 20cm round cake tin lined with non-stick baking paper on the bottom and the sides. Bake for 40 minutes in a preheated oven set at 180°C.

Meanwhile, mix the topping ingredients together until well combined and set aside until required.

Test the cake and when a skewer inserted into the centre comes out clean remove cake from the oven and increase the heat to 225°C. Spread the topping over the cake and return to the oven and bake for 10–15 minutes at 225°C until the topping is baked through.

Remove the cake from the oven and cool for 10 minutes in the tin before transferring to a cooling rack.

dark devil's food chocolate cupcakes

make 24 medium muffin-sized cupcakes

These little devils have a whole lot of indulgence packed into every mouthful — sinful, indeed! Cupcakes are the 'in' thing and these are perfect in size and shape. Many people make cupcakes the size of huge muffins but I prefer to keep them smaller.

215g plain flour
2 teaspoons baking powder
¾ teaspoon baking soda
½ teaspoon salt
155g unsalted butter, softened
300g granulated sugar
60g Dutch cocoa

2 eggs
1 teaspoon vanilla essence
280ml warm water

silver cachous, sweets cut in half
  or sprinkles for decoration

Sift the flour, baking powder, baking soda and salt together into a large bowl and set aside until required.

Put the butter into the bowl of an electric mixer fitted with a beater and begin to mix on medium speed for 1–2 minutes until light and creamy. Pour in the sugar in a steady stream while continuing to beat on slow speed. Once it has all been added increase the speed to high and beat for 3 minutes or until pale, light and fluffy. Add the cocoa powder and mix for a further 1 minute on medium speed. Scrape down the sides of the bowl. Beat in the eggs one at a time and beat well after each addition.

Add the vanilla and continuing to beat on low speed, add the dry ingredients in three equal amounts, alternating with half the warm water. Scrape down the bowl and beat on low speed for a further 30 seconds.

Spoon the batter into 24 medium muffin cups lined with cupcake papers so each cup is just over half full. Bake in a preheated oven set at 180°C for approximately 25 minutes or until the cakes are springy and a little firm to the touch. Allow to cool for 10 minutes in their cups before transferring to a cooling rack. When completely cool, ice with ganache icing (see below).

ganache icing (makes enough for 12 cupcakes)
200ml fresh cream
400g milk or dark chocolate (good quality)

Bring the cream to the boil. Remove from the heat and add the chocolate and stir until melted and there are no lumps left. Continue stirring as the ganache cools and when it has reached piping consistency — when it almost holds stiff peaks — transfer it to a piping bag fitted with a plain or star piping tube. Pipe a circular spiral or rosette on top of each cupcake and decorate according to taste. For example; you might use silver cachous for a favourite aunt and brightly coloured sweets for a niece or nephew.

spiced summer berry compote muffins

makes 12 standard muffins

Summer berries and spices — what better way to top off a lovely muffin? And there are more berries hidden inside each muffin. The thing I love about this recipe is you can add almost any flavours you want. You can use a mixture of berries and small fruit, such as raspberries, blueberries and redcurrants. If they are not available, try other fruit — fresh stonefruit would be delicious with or without the spices.

spiced summer berry compote

350g mixed frozen berries
50g caster sugar
¼ teaspoon Chinese five spice powder

2 teaspoons cornflour, mixed with
 1 tablespoon water

Heat three quarters of the frozen fruit together with the sugar and five spice powder until it just begins to boil. Add the cornflour and cook until it thickens. Try not to crush the fruit with excessive stirring — you want to keep it whole if possible. Remove from the heat and add the rest of the frozen berries and stir to combine. Set aside in a bowl until required.

muffins

450g plain flour
50g wholemeal flour
340g caster sugar
25g baking powder
5g Chinese five spice powder
410ml milk
5 small size eggs

100g vegetable oil, such as canola oil
100g butter, melted
1 teaspoon vanilla extract
250g frozen mixed berries

icing sugar for dusting

Sift the flours, sugar, baking powder and five spice powder together into a large bowl and set aside. Using a hand whisk, whisk the milk, eggs, oil, butter and vanilla extract together, but do not incorporate too much air into the mix.

Using a wooden spoon, combine the wet and dry ingredients until the batter just comes together and there is still a little flour showing. Add the mixed berries and gently fold into the batter, taking care not to over-mix — if you do the baked muffins will be tough.

Spoon the batter into 12 standard muffin cups lined with cupcake papers so each cup is just over half full. Bake in a preheated oven set at 190°C for 30–35 minutes until springy and a little firm to the touch. Allow to cool for 10 minutes in their tins before transferring to a cooling rack. To serve, dust with icing sugar and top each muffin with a large teaspoonful of spiced summer berry compote — don't worry if some of the juice runs down the side of the muffins.

dairy-free banana & walnut soya muffin

makes 12 standard muffins

Finally a muffin that is good for you — this one is dairy-free and has all the health benefits of soy milk. Of course you can change the flavour, but banana and walnut work particularly well with soy milk. The glazed top and ring of toasted thread coconut around the edge make them look stunning.

450g plain flour
50g wholemeal flour
340g caster sugar
25g baking powder
330ml soy milk
5 small size eggs
200g vegetable oil, such as canola oil

1 teaspoon vanilla extract
120g banana, mashed
100g walnuts, chopped

100g walnuts, finely chopped,
    for topping
24 slices of banana for topping

apricot glaze (see page 242)
100g thread coconut, toasted at 190°C until amber in colour for decorating

Sift the flours, sugar and baking powder together into a large bowl and set aside. Using a hand whisk, whisk the soy milk, eggs, oil, vanilla, mashed banana and walnuts together in another bowl, but do not incorporate too much air into the mix.

Using a wooden spoon, combine the wet and dry ingredients until the batter just comes together and there is still a little flour showing taking care not to over-mix — if you do the baked muffins will be tough.

Spoon the batter into 12 standard muffin cups lined with cupcake papers so each cup is just over half full. Sprinkle walnuts on top and press 2 slices of banana into each muffin. Bake in a preheated oven set at 190°C for approximately 30–35 minutes until springy and a little firm to the touch. Allow to cool for 10 minutes in their cups before transferring to a cooling rack.

To serve, heat the apricot glaze and brush the entire top surface of each muffin with glaze and sprinkle the outer edge with a ring of toasted coconut.

sticky stem-ginger cake with lemon icing & ginger-syrup infused greek yoghurt

makes 1x20cm round cake

Emma Freeman made this as her signature baked product on the first episode of 'Nestlé New Zealand's Hottest Home Baker'. It was drop-dead gorgeous — I adore ginger cake anyway, but this was a real winner.

225g self-raising flour
1 teaspoon baking soda
1 tablespoon ground ginger
1 teaspoon cinnamon
1 teaspoon mixed spice
115g butter
115g dark muscovado sugar

115g treacle
115g golden syrup
250ml milk
85g stem ginger in syrup, drained, grated and syrup reserved
1 egg, lightly beaten

Sift the flour, baking soda and spices into a food processor and add the butter. Pulse to form fine crumbs and transfer to a large mixing bowl until required.

Heat the muscovado sugar, treacle, golden syrup and milk together, stirring until the sugar has dissolved. Turn up the heat and bring mixture to just below boiling then remove from the heat. Add the stem ginger and warm sugar and milk mixture to the dry ingredients and stir together until almost combined. Add the egg and beat the mixture until well combined. Pour into a 20cm round cake tin lined with non-stick baking paper and bake for 50 minutes–1 hour in a preheated oven set at 180°C until a skewer inserted in the centre of the cake comes out clean. Remove from the oven and leave to cool in the tin.

When cool, drizzle with lemon icing (see below) and serve with Greek yoghurt flavoured with the syrup from the stem ginger syrup.

lemon icing

This simple lemon icing is perfect for drizzling on cakes of all flavours, but is especially good with ginger, banana, berry and coconut concoctions.

100g icing sugar, sifted
2 teaspoons lemon zest

1 tablespoon lemon juice

Mix the icing sugar and zest together and gradually add the lemon juice, mixing to form a smooth and runny icing suitable for drizzling.

luxury milo fruit & nut slice

makes 24 pieces

When I was growing up, lolly cake made with malt biscuits, condensed milk, butter and fruit puffs was a regular feature in the cake tin at home. This is my grown-up take on a childhood favourite. Starting with a baked shortcrust base, the dried fruit and nuts give the topping a little kick and the ganache and toasted-coconut icing provides contrast. Take care not to cut this too big — it's a very rich slice ideal for serving with coffee.

slice

1 batch sweet pastry (see page 224)

50g pine nuts

50g thread coconut

250g sweetened condensed milk

150g butter, softened

100g Milo powder

250g wine biscuits or similar, crushed to fine crumbs

50g pistachio nuts, roughly chopped

50g pecans roughly chopped, but not too small

50g sultanas

70g figs, stems removed, each fig cut into 6 pieces

70g dried apricots, each apricot cut into 5 pieces

70g dried cranberries

70g crystallised ginger

1 batch light ganache (see opposite)

30g toasted thread coconut for decorating

On a floured bench, roll the sweet pastry out to 4mm thick and line the base of a 27 x 17 x 3cm slice tin lined with non-stick baking paper. Wrap the leftover pastry in plastic wrap and place in the freezer for another day. Prick the pastry with a fork all over and bake for 15 minutes in a preheated oven set at 180°C or until light golden brown.

While the base is baking, toast the pine nuts for the slice and the thread coconut for decorating the light ganache topping until lightly golden.

Remove coconut, pine nuts and base from the oven and set aside to cool until required. Carefully remove the shortcrust base and transfer to a cooling rack. When cooled, return the shortcrust back into the tin. Set aside until required.

Stir the condensed milk and butter together over a low heat until the butter has melted. Remove from the heat and stir in the Milo. Set aside until required.

In a separate large mixing bowl, place the biscuit crumbs, toasted coconut, nuts, dried fruits and ginger. Pour in the Milo mixture and mix thoroughly. Press the mixture firmly into the prepared slice tray making sure it is level. Cover with plastic wrap and place in the refrigerator for at least 4 hours until firm.

Remove the slice from the refrigerator and take off the plastic wrap. Using a palette knife, spread the light ganache (see opposite) onto the slice and immediately sprinkle the toasted thread coconut on top. Return to the refrigerator for at least 1 hour to allow the icing to set. Carefully remove the slice from the tin and place onto a chopping board. Using a knife dipped in hot water, cut into even-sized squares, rectangles or triangles, as desired.

light ganache

80ml fresh cream   20g milk chocolate

150g white chocolate

Bring the cream to the boil. Remove from the heat and add the chocolate and stir until melted and there are no lumps left. Continue stirring as the ganache cools and when it has reached a spreading consistency use immediately.

berry stella healthy tart

makes 9 stars or 10cm round tarts

This is neither a cookie nor a muffin — it's somewhere in between. It can be baked in individual shaped tins or moulds or made in a slice tin and cut into squares or rectangles. There is a healthy side to this treat with all the flours, oats, seeds and natural fruits. I love the star shape as it adds something extra in eye appeal.

tart base

225g plain flour

50g wholemeal flour

80g rolled oats, if possible select large oats that are not too flattened

50g sunflower seeds

50g sesame seeds

50g linseeds

150g sugar

60g brown sugar

10g baking powder

¼ teaspoon cinnamon

3 eggs

75g vegetable oil

75g softened butter

2 tablespoons water

30g honey

topping

40g jumbo rolled oats

70g frozen blueberries

70g frozen redcurrants, raspberries or blueberries

apricot glaze (see page 242), heated

To make the base, put all the dry ingredients in the bowl of an electric mixer fitted with beater attachments and beat on low speed for 3 minutes or until well combined. Add the remaining ingredients and continue to mix for 2–3 minutes to form something that resembles a cookie dough.

Form the dough into 100g balls and flatten into moulds, if using, or spread into a 27 x 17 x 3cm slice tin lined with baking paper. Make sure the surface is flat. Lightly sprinkle the surface with the toppings in the order listed and gently push them into the surface.

Place into a preheated oven set at 180°C and bake for about 30–35 minutes until slightly golden brown in colour. Remove from the oven and cool for 10 minutes. Transfer from the moulds or slice tin to a cooling rack and glaze with hot apricot glaze. If you are using a slice tray then glaze in the tray and cut when cool.

almond frangipane fruit tartlets

makes 6 tarts

These little tarts are easy and, better still, the bases can be prepared a few days in advance and kept in the freezer, then thawed the day you need them. You can add whatever topping you want, so don't limit yourself to the ones I've suggested. Serve tartlets as a dessert with ice cream and a fruit sauce.

tarts

1 batch sweet pastry (see page 224), chilled
120g softened butter
120g sugar
2 large eggs, whisked together and slightly warmed
100g ground almonds
15g plain flour
1 tablespoon Amaretto liqueur (optional)

toppings

50g frozen mixed berries
100g frozen or fresh raw rhubarb, cut into 1cm pieces
1 small apricot, cut in half, destoned and sliced lengthways
30g thread coconut, lightly toasted
50g almonds flakes, lightly toasted and crushed
30g pistachio nuts, roughly chopped

apricot glaze (see page 242)

On a lightly floured work surface, roll out the sweet pastry to 3mm thick. Cut circles slightly larger than the 6 tart shells you are using — 10cm diameter is about right. Line the tart shells and trim the top edges with a sharp knife.

To make the filling, beat the butter and sugar together in a mixing bowl with a wooden spoon until light and creamy. Add the eggs bit by bit to avoid curdling and beat well after each addition until well combined. Add the ground almonds, flour and Amaretto liqueur, if using, and continue beating to form a smooth cream-like consistency.

Using a small spoon, place a small amount of the filling in the bottom of each tart shell — they should be about three-quarters full.

Making two of each kind, arrange the 3 toppings — berries, rhubarb, apricot — on the cream filling and press them very gently so they are in the mixture but still quite exposed.

Place in a preheated oven set at 200°C and bake for 30–35 minutes until lightly golden on the top. Remove from the oven and cool for 10 minutes in the tins. Transfer to a cooling rack and brush the tops with hot apricot glaze. Before the glaze has set, sprinkle the berry tarts with toasted thread coconut, the rhubarb tarts with toasted flaked almonds and the apricot tarts with chopped pistachio nuts. Or you can decorate as you see fit.

black sesame seed-crusted vegetarian quiche

makes 1x20cm round quiche

To make a vegetarian quiche I usually open the fridge and see what's in there to combine with spices, herbs, chilli or whatever else takes my fancy at the time. The black sesame seeds in this crust look terrific — you should find them easily enough at your local Asian supermarket. Remember to keep the pastry thin and bake it blind before filling — there's nothing worse than a thick, soggy pastry base.

1 batch black sesame seed short
  pastry (see page 227), chilled
100g pumpkin, deseeded, peeled
  and cut into 1cm cubes
olive oil
100g leeks, washed and sliced
75g fennel, sliced about 5mm thick
3 asparagus spears, cut into 2cm
  lengths
50g button mushrooms
a knob of butter
pepper and salt

50g sour cream
3 eggs
100ml cream
2 tablespoon wholegrain mustard
freshly grated nutmeg
100g feta cheese, cut into 1cm cubes
6–8 cherry tomatoes, each sliced
  into 3
70g pine nuts, toasted until amber
  in colour
leaves from 2 sprigs of fresh thyme

On a lightly floured work surface, roll out the pastry to 3mm thick. Line the base and sides of a 20cm round, fluted loose-bottomed flan tin or a 35cm x 10cm fluted loose-bottomed rectangular tart tin. Place in the refrigerator for 30 minutes. Preheat the oven to 200°C, line the pastry with tinfoil and fill with dried beans, raw rice or pastry weights. Bake blind for 20–25 minutes until it is lightly coloured. Remove the tinfoil and pastry weights.

Toss the pumpkin in a little olive oil and roast at 200°C until tender while the pastry is cooking.

One at a time, sauté the leeks, fennel, asparagus and mushrooms in a little butter until just tender and season with salt and pepper.

Whisk the sour cream in a mixing bowl until smooth. Add the eggs and whisk together until combined. Add the cream, mustard and a good grind of nutmeg and whisk until combined — do not over whisk at this stage.

Toss the vegetables together and spread them into the pre-baked pastry case. Pour the egg mixture evenly over the vegetables, taking care not to spill any mixture over the side. Scatter the feta, tomatoes, pine nuts and thyme randomly over the top of the filling and bake for 20–25 minutes in a preheated oven set at 180°C until the mixture is just set and firm to the touch. Remove from the oven and allow to cool in the tin.

almond & rosemary biscotti

makes 25 small biscotti

Biscotti are simple to make — they're just cookie bars lightly baked in a log that's sliced and the slices are baked again. You can make them with many different flavour combinations, but this almond and rosemary combo is great with coffee.

75g almonds, blanched (skins removed)
75g fine caster sugar
100g plain flour
¾ teaspoon baking powder
1 egg

½ teaspoon softened butter
¼ teaspoon vanilla essence
1 teaspoon finely chopped fresh
  rosemary leaves

Roast the almonds in a preheated oven set at 180°C until pale golden. Remove from the oven and set aside to cool.

Sift the sugar, flour and baking powder together in a large bowl and add the remaining ingredients. Using a wooden spoon, beat together to form a dough mass.

With floured hands, divide the dough in half and on a lightly floured surface, roll each half of the dough into a log shape 3–5cm wide. Place the logs 5cm apart on a baking sheet lined with non-stick baking paper. Bake in a preheated oven set at 170°C for 20 minutes or until firm to the touch. Remove from the oven and transfer to a cooling rack for 10 minutes or until cool enough to handle.

Transfer logs to a cutting board and using a serrated knife, cut logs on the diagonal into slices ½ cm thick. Arrange evenly on the paper-lined baking tray. Turn the oven down to 120°C and bake for 10 minutes, turn slices over, and bake for another 10 minutes or until firm to the touch. Remove from the oven and transfer to a cooling rack. Store in an airtight container until required.

From top left, going clockwise: Mini Belgian Biscuits, Almond & Rosemary Biscotti, Love Heart Jam Dodgers, Strawberries & Cream Truffles, and in centre, Tropical Passionfruit & Coconut Chocolate Truffles.

tropical passionfruit & coconut chocolate truffles

makes 40–45 truffles

Passionfruit and coconut are amazing together. The seeds are included to give a wee crackle when you bite into the truffles, but they can easily be omitted if you don't like them. I like to use Belgian chocolate for these.

80ml fresh cream

20g unsalted butter

130g dark chocolate, broken
   into chunks

130g milk chocolate, broken
   into chunks

50ml passionfruit pulp, including

the seeds, if liked

75g thread coconut

250g good-quality cocoa powder

icing sugar to powder hands

350g dark chocolate, melted, for rolling
   truffles

Heat the cream and butter in a heavy-based saucepan to 90°C — just below boiling point. Remove the saucepan from the heat and add the broken chocolate, passionfruit pulp and coconut and stir until chocolate has melted. Pour the mixture into a medium-sized plastic container and place in the refrigerator for 1–2 hours.

Sieve the cocoa into a shallow tray and set aside.

Remove the truffle mixture from the refrigerator and use a teaspoon to scoop out heaped spoonfuls of truffle mixture.

Powder the palms of your hands with icing sugar and roll each spoonful of truffle mix into a ball. Place balls on a sheet of greaseproof paper. Place in the refrigerator for at least 1 hour until firm.

Cover your hands with melted chocolate, and roll the balls in the palms of your hands, making sure to get a thin, even covering of chocolate around each ball then place them in the cocoa powder and roll them around to ensure an even coating of cocoa powder over the chocolate. Place the balls on greaseproof paper to set and store in an airtight container in the refrigerator until required. Remove the truffles from the refrigerator 30 minutes before serving.

love heart jam dodgers

makes 12 biscuit sandwiches

These are a play on a very popular biscuit from the United Kingdom. They are cute and will bring a smile to your partner's face on Valentine's Day.

1 batch sweet pastry (see page 224), chilled
100g good quality redcurrant or raspberry jam

icing sugar for dusting

On a lightly floured bench roll the pastry out to 3–4 mm thick. Using a small heart-shaped cutter approximately 5cm x 3cm, cut out 24 hearts and place on a baking tray lined with non-stick baking paper approximately 1cm apart. Using a much smaller heart-shaped cutter cut the centres out of 12 of the biscuits so you have 12 heart-shaped frames.

Bake for 10–12 minutes in a preheated oven set at 180°C until lightly golden in colour and firm to touch. Transfer to a cooling rack. Using a fine sieve, dust the frames with icing sugar. Turn over the solid heart biscuits and spread ½ teaspoon of jam on each biscuit. Place a frame on top of each base and very gently press down.

strawberries & cream truffles

makes 50 truffles

Can anyone resist strawberries and cream? The key to these truffles is the dried strawberries. Choose ripe ones and the flavour will be intense.

dried strawberries

5 fresh strawberries

200g caster sugar

275ml water

Cut the hull out of the strawberries and discard. Wash and dry the strawberries, then thinly slice them.

Bring the sugar and water to the boil in a large heavy-based saucepan. Remove from the heat and pour into a bowl and cool slightly.

Plunge the strawberry slices into the syrup and leave to soak overnight in the refrigerator. The next day drain the strawberry slices and carefully dry both sides on paper towels. Place on a baking tray lined with non-stick baking paper and bake for 1 hour in a preheated oven set at 100°C. Turn the slices over after 30 minutes. They should be dry and crisp when removed from the oven.

Allow to cool completely then chop into small pieces. Store in an airtight container.

truffles

80ml fresh cream

20g unsalted butter

260g white chocolate, broken
   into chunks

1 batch dried strawberries

icing sugar to powder hands

350g white chocolate, melted,
   for rolling truffles

Heat the cream and butter in a heavy-based saucepan to 90°C — just below boiling point. Remove the saucepan from the heat and add the broken chocolate and stir until the chocolate has melted. Allow to cool but while it is still liquid, add the dried strawberry pieces. Pour the mixture into a medium-sized plastic container and place in the refrigerator for 1–2 hours.

Remove the truffle mixture from the refrigerator and use a teaspoon to scoop out heaped spoonfuls of truffle mixture. Powder the palms of your hands with icing sugar and roll the spoonfuls of truffle mix into balls. Place balls on a sheet of greaseproof paper. Place in the refrigerator for at least 1 hour until firm.

Cover the palms of your hands with melted chocolate, then roll each ball in melted chocolate making sure to get a thin, even covering of chocolate around each ball. Place the balls on greaseproof paper to set and then repeat the covering process. Store in an airtight container in a refrigerator.

mini belgian biscuits

makes 15 biscuit sandwiches

The biscuits are made like a sweet pastry but the fragrant spices, ground hazelnuts, hint of lemon zest and the fresh and fruity jam provide richness. You can keep the pastry in the freezer to thaw and bake as required.

biscuit dough

115g butter, softened
85g caster sugar
zest of $\frac{1}{2}$ a lemon
few drops of vanilla extract or essence
1 egg, lightly beaten
150g plain flour
$\frac{1}{4}$ teaspoon baking powder

$\frac{1}{4}$ teaspoon ground cinnamon
$\frac{1}{8}$ teaspoon ground cloves
$\frac{1}{2}$ teaspoon cocoa powder
20g white sponge crumbs
55g hazelnuts, finely ground and
    lightly toasted

icing and decoration

75g icing sugar
$\frac{1}{4}$–$\frac{1}{2}$ teaspoon water
red food colouring

50g fine sugar
100g good quality redcurrant or
    raspberry jam for filling

Using a wooden spoon, beat the butter, sugar, lemon zest and vanilla together in a medium-sized mixing bowl until pale and fluffy. Lightly beat the egg and add half at a time to the creamed mixture beating well after each addition. Mix the flour, baking powder, cinnamon, cloves, cocoa, cake crumbs and ground hazelnuts together and add to the creamed mixture. Mix to form a dough ball. Wrap with plastic wrap and place in the refrigerator for 1 hour or overnight to firm up.

Remove dough from the refrigerator and on a lightly floured bench, roll out to 3mm thick. Using a 3cm plain or crinkled round cutter, cut 30 circles and place them 1cm apart on a baking tray lined with non-stick baking paper. Bake for 10–12 minutes in a preheated oven set at 180°C until lightly golden in colour and firm to touch. Remove from the oven and transfer to a cooling rack.

To make the icing, mix the icing sugar together with the water a few drops at a time to a spreading consistency.

Add the food colouring, one drop at a time, to the fine sugar and rub together with your fingers until the desired colour is achieved.

To finish, turn over 15 cooled biscuits and spread $\frac{1}{2}$ teaspoon of jam on each. Place another biscuit on top of each base and very gently press down. Spoon a drop of white icing on top and spread to form a small circle. Sprinkle some pink sugar in the centre of the white icing.

marshmallows in a sesame seed brandy snap puddle

makes 50 marshmallows and 1 brandy snap puddle

This recipe gives you a 'melt in the mouth' sensation you don't get from mass-produced marshmallows. Choose lots of different flavours and colours. The edible puddle is a fun way to serve these petits fours. This is guaranteed to be a hit at kids' parties, too. You'll need a sugar thermometer.

marshmallows

20g powdered gelatine
180ml cold water
2 egg whites
240g sugar
240g liquid glucose
90ml water

colouring and flavoured essences
    of your choice
100g icing sugar for coating
    marshmallow cubes
100g cornflour for coating marshmallow
    cubes

Soak the gelatine in the cold water for 10 minutes. Place over a saucepan of simmering hot water to dissolve.

Place the egg whites into the clean grease-free bowl of an electric mixer fitted with a whisk attachment and whisk on low speed to form stiff peaks.

Bring the sugar, liquid glucose and water to the boil and continue heating to 127°C. Remove from the heat and while the egg whites are still whisking on low speed, slowly pour the hot syrup into the egg whites. Add the melted gelatine and a few drops of colouring and flavoured essence and continue to whisk until the marshmallow becomes stiff and thick. Spread into a slice tin lined with non-stick baking paper. Smooth out the top with a palette knife or straight-edged plastic scraper.

Sift the icing sugar and cornflour together and sprinkle over the marshmallow. Cover and leave overnight to set at room temperature. Cut marshmallow into cubes and toss in the excess icing sugar and cornflour mixture to coat each cube.

brandy snap puddle

45g butter
30g golden syrup
35g sugar
20g plain flour
½ teaspoon ground ginger

3 teaspoons white sesame seeds,
    lightly toasted
3 teaspoons black sesame seeds,
    lightly toasted

Put the butter, golden syrup and sugar in a bowl set over a saucepan of simmering water until melted together. Remove from the heat. Sift the flour and ginger together and add the sesame seeds. Add to the wet mixture and stir to combine.

Arrange the mixture in a tear drop shape — 30cm long x 15cm wide at one end tapering off to 5cm at the other end — on a baking tray lined with non-stick baking paper. Bake for 5 minutes in a preheated oven set at 180°C or until dark golden brown all the way through. Remove from the oven, and allow to cool slightly before picking it up and bending it over a large upturned bowl so that it sets like a shell with a large flat base. Allow to cool. To serve, carefully place the brandy snap bowl onto a large serving plate and arrange the marshmallows on it.

basics

basic baking techniques

steps in mixing or kneading bread dough by hand

Mixing or kneading should be fun and enjoyable, not something that is hard work or that is hurried. Ensure that you knead on a solid surface with plenty of space, and that the bench is of suitable height.

The secret to easy hand kneading is to take a small rest of approximately 30 seconds to 1 minute during the kneading process. This allows for the elastic and extensible flour proteins to relax a little before further kneading and manipulation and, also importantly, allows you a small rest too. You will find hand kneading much more enjoyable when using this method and you will not tire so quickly.

1. Place the flour into a large bowl and then sprinkle the other ingredients around the outside.

2. Slowly add the water and other liquids into the middle of the bowl of dry ingredients. Always keep a small amount of water back to adjust the dough to the correct consistency.

3. Using a wooden spoon or your hand, mix in the liquids, using a circular motion, until all the ingredients have come together in one mass.

4. Tip the dough mass onto a lightly floured work surface ready for kneading. Have a small bowl of flour handy for lightly dusting the bench during the kneading process.

5. At this stage begin to knead the dough by using both hands to lift it upwards and then folding it back onto itself (to stretch the dough and trap the air in it). Repeat this procedure for 1-2 minutes, then allow the dough to rest untouched for 2-3 minutes, to allow the protein strands to recover and relax.

6. Note: The dough will be sticky and rough in texture at this stage. Don't worry, it will get better. All recipes in this book should take almost the exact amount of liquid and only minor adjustments should be necessary.

7. Continue to knead the dough using the method described. This should take about 15 minutes and your dough should become smooth, silky and elastic.

8. Let the dough rest every 2-3 minutes during the kneading process and you will find it will become smooth, silky and elastic faster.

understanding when a dough is fully mixed

As discussed, in mixing and kneading, this is one of the most important steps in successful bread making. Good bread flour contains a protein called gluten, which gives structure and strength to all yeast-raised goods.

In order for gluten to be developed, the proteins (glutenin and gliadin) must first absorb water or liquids, then as the dough is mixed or kneaded the gluten forms long, elastic and rubbery strands, known as the gluten network.

As the dough begins to rise the gluten network captures the gases (produced by the yeast) in tiny pockets or cells and this allows the dough to rise and expand. If the gluten network within the dough has not been correctly developed these gases will escape into the air, resulting in a collapsed small-volume loaf.

There are many factors that determine when a dough is fully mixed:
- temperature of water
- speed of kneading
- selection and amounts of raw ingredients (high-fat and sugar doughs take less time to mix due to the 'shortening' and 'softening' effect these ingredients have on the gluten network).

The dough is fully mixed when:
- the dough has a smooth, silky and elastic texture. A rough and easily broken dough is still under-mixed and needs a lot more mixing.
- a small piece of dough can be stretched to achieve a smooth satiny sheen which is elastic and extensible (often called the stretch test).

1. An under-developed dough. Notice the rough and easily broken texture of the dough when stretched out.

2. A correctly developed dough: smooth, elastic and extensible when stretched.

other bread making terms

bulk fermentation
Also known as first rising. This term is used to describe the length of time that the dough is allowed to ferment in bulk. The bulk fermentation period is measured from the end of mixing to the beginning of scaling or dividing the dough. This period can be from 1–18 hours depending on the levels of salt and yeast in the recipe, as well as the dough temperature, which should be between 25 and 27°C.

During bulk fermentation the following conditions must be observed:
- place the dough into a lightly oiled container large enough to allow the dough to double in size
- the dough must be covered to prevent the dough surface from skinning
- place the dough in an environment where the temperature will remain constant (in the domestic environment, place the covered dough in the hot water cupboard).

knocking back/deflating the dough
During the bulk fermentation period the dough increases in volume (often doubling). This is caused by the gases given off by the yeast. To avoid the gases from escaping prematurely the dough is gently 'knocked back', generally three-quarters of the way through the bulk fermentation period. This is done by hand, by very gently pushing and folding the dough. Knocking back is done for the following reasons:
- to expel the gases and revitalise the yeast's activity
- to even out the dough temperature because the outside of the dough will be colder than the inside
- to stimulate and help develop strength of the gluten network
- to even out the cell structure.

Once the knocking back stage has been completed the dough is returned to the container and covered until it is required for scaling. Bulk fermentation and knocking back times are included in the relevant recipes within this book.

dividing or scaling
Dough dividing or scaling takes place as soon as the dough has completed either its mixing or bulk fermentation period. This is simply done by using scales and dough scraper. Gently divide the dough into the required sizes and weights. This should be done as quickly as possible to avoid excessive fermentation of the dough.

rounding
After scaling, the dough pieces are shaped into smooth, round balls. This assists the gases within the fermenting dough to remain inside rather than escaping into the air. Another reason why this stage is important is that it's when the dough is pre-shaped into uniform pieces before it undergoes its final shaping. To achieve this cup your hand or hands over

the dough piece and with a little pressure begin to move your dough in a circular motion making sure that the dough is in contact with the bench all the time. Avoid rounding on a floured surface as you want the dough to grip the bench. This movement stretches the surface of the dough so that it is completely smooth except for a seam at the bottom where the dough has gripped the bench.

intermediate proof

Sometimes referred to as 'first proof', 'recovery time' or 'bench time'. This is a resting period of 10–15 minutes that takes place between rounding and final make up or shaping, allowing the gluten network to relax. If insufficient intermediate proof time is given the dough piece will tear and become misshapen during final make up or shaping. During the intermediate proof you must cover your dough pieces with either a sheet of plastic wrap, dough cloth or simply a clean tea towel to avoid the dough surface from skinning.

final moulding and placing on trays

Once the dough piece has had its intermediate proof it is time to mould it into its final shape before it is placed directly into bread tins, proofing baskets or onto baking trays. Correct make up or moulding is critical to the finished baked loaf or roll. All moulded bread doughs have a seam, and the seam should always be placed bottom side down on trays and in tins. This avoids splitting during the baking process (with the exception of cane proofing baskets where the smooth surface should be placed at the bottom).

Once the final shaping has taken place, toppings can be put onto the dough piece before it enters the final proof stage, eg. sesame and poppy seeds, cheese, flour.

There are many effective shapes that breads, rolls and buns can take. Many are shown in recipes within this book.

1. Moulding a round cob or boule loaf. Turn the scrunched up bottom onto the work surface, cup your hands over and move in a circular motion until a tight skin is formed.

2. Moulding for tin bread. Mould long then roll into a tight pinwheel log. Place into a tin, seam side down.

3. Moulding flat tray bread (baguettes) with pointed tapered ends. Use your thumb and heel of your hand to make a tight seal.

4. Moulding a round ball for dinner rolls or buns.

final proof

Often known as 'proofing'. This is critical for product quality and should be monitored closely. Once the dough is ready to enter the prover there are three main areas that require attention. They are as follows:

- Temperature. Proofing temperatures should be higher than the dough temperature. This prevents the dough from chilling and allows the yeast to function effectively. The ideal temperature should be between 35 and 40°C.
- Humidity. The requirement for humidity in final proofing is to prevent the drying of the dough piece. Skinning prevents a glossy crust forming during steaming and baking. Lack of humidity will slow proofing. Higher humidity will result in excessive heat (as humidity is produced by steam) and this could cause par-baked product. In the domestic environment a spray bottle can be used to prevent skinning during proofing.
- Time. Proof times depend on dough size, final dough temperature, yeast levels and even ingredients used. Common proof times are 45–90 minutes.

If a prover is not available, create conditions as close as possible to the above by covering the products loosely to retain the moisture and setting them in a warm place (in a hot water cupboard or similar).

using the indentation test to check proof time

under-proofed

This is when you lightly press your finger into the side of the dough and the indentation springs out quickly to its original shape. More proof time is required.

correct proof

Lightly press your finger into the side of the dough and, this time, the indentation slowly springs back, but does not go back to its original shape. It leaves a small indentation mark. At this stage, the dough piece is ready to enter the oven.

over-proofed

When lightly pressed, the dough piece will collapse and the indentation mark will not spring back. Place the dough piece directly into the oven as soon as possible at the correct oven temperature, but the product will be of poor quality.

cutting, seeding and dusting

Generally done for the decorative appearance of a finished baked loaf or roll.

- cutting or slashing is done with a razor blade or sharp slashing knife. Always cut the dough at three-quarter proof.
- seeding is done either after the final shaping or just before the fully proofed loaf or rolls enter the oven. If the latter is done then the loaf or rolls need to be lightly

sprayed with water before the seeds are sprinkled on to allow the seeds to adhere to the surface of the dough. Grated cheese etc can also be applied at this stage.

· dusting the loaf or rolls with flour at full proof allows the flour to bake onto the product.

Dusting and cutting are normally done together to achieve a decorative pattern.

baking

The final and most important step in transforming the unpalatable pale, wet, plastic-like dough into a light, porous, digestible and flavoursome product for consumption. Proofed doughs are fragile until the flour proteins have been coagulated (set) by the baking process. The dough should be handled with care when being loaded into the preheated oven. The heat causes the yeast, in the last stages of life, to lift the dough one more time before it is killed by the excessive heat. This is called oven spring. For this to happen the oven must be hot and moist. Professional bakers use steam injected ovens which prevent the crust from drying out and being dull in colour. For a domestic oven, use a water spray bottle to spray the sides and baking stone with warm water one minute before inserting the dough piece, then repeat this 2 or 3 times within the first 5 minutes of baking. Alternatively, have an ovenproof dish in the bottom of the oven and throw 4 or 5 cubes of ice into it to create instant steam. Ensure that you only open the door slightly each time you spray, to avoid excessive steam- and heat-loss. Once your dough piece is in the oven avoid spraying it directly with the water, as this will cause an inferior finished product.

baking on the baking stones or the hearth of the oven.
To load the oven, place the proofed dough piece or pieces onto peels that have been well dusted with semolina or cornmeal. Slide the peel into the oven, then with a quick forward and backward jerk slide the dough piece onto the baking stone or hearth of the oven.

baking on trays or in tins.
Many products such as rolls, buns and tin breads, are baked on trays or in tins which are directly placed onto the baking stones or the hearth of the oven, however these are not known as traditional hearth breads. Baking the ideal product is dependent on time, temperature and dough weight.

· large dough pieces (400–500 grams) require high temperatures and longer baking periods, ie. 220–230°C for 30–40 minutes.
· small dough pieces (100–200 grams) require significantly less time and lower baking temperatures, ie. 200–210°C for 12–18 minutes.

baking guidelines

The longer the baking time:
· the thicker the crust
· the greater the moisture loss
· the darker the crust colour

The higher the baking temperature:
· the shorter the baking time
· the thinner the product crust
· the more risk that the larger dough pieces
     will be under baked and may collapse

The lower the baking temperature:
· the longer the total baking time
· the thicker the product crust
· the more oven spring

To tell if a loaf of bread is correctly baked, tap the bottom and if it makes a hollow sound the loaf is correctly baked.

cooling

After baking the loaves and rolls they must be left to cool. The flavour and aroma don't fully develop until the loaf has cooled completely. Always place your baked breads directly onto a cooling rack or wire to prevent sweating after baking. Allow the bread to cool completely before slicing or cutting as this will ensure even slicing can be achieved and the texture will be shown to its full potential.

storing

Breads to be served within 8 hours may be left in the open air or in a paper bag. Breads that are to retain a crust must not be packaged, as this would cause the crusts to soften and become leathery. If storing your bread in the freezer, place it in a plastic bag to extend its shelf life. Never place bread in the refrigerator as this causes it to go stale quickly.

basic white or sandwich bread

300g bread flour
5g salt
5g sugar
1/2 teaspoon instant dried yeast

10g olive oil
185ml water
4 small knobs of butter

Place all the ingredients into a large mixing bowl and, using a wooden spoon, combine the ingredients until a dough mass has formed. Tip the dough out onto a lightly floured surface and knead for 15–20 minutes (taking a 30-second rest every 3–4 minutes) until the dough is smooth and elastic in feel. This will take a while as the dough will be sticky to the touch, but don't be tempted to add excessive amounts of flour during the kneading process — a little will be okay, but please persevere with the softness.

Lightly oil a bowl large enough to allow the dough to double in bulk, then put the dough into the bowl and cover with plastic wrap. Leave in a warmish place (23–25°C) for 1 hour. Gently knock back the dough in the bowl by gently folding it back onto itself. This will deflate it slightly, but it will develop more strength. Cover again with plastic wrap and leave for 30 minutes.

Next, tip the dough out onto a lightly floured bench, flatten and mould it into a rectangular loaf shape and place into a greased 500g (1lb) loaf tin. Cover the loaf with a sheet of plastic and proof for 60 minutes.

Using a sharp knife or razor blade cut straight down the centre of the loaf lengthways and place 4 small knobs of butter down the length of the cut.

Place into a preheated oven set at 200–210°C. Have a small ovenproof dish ready on the bottom shelf, then quickly throw 3 or 4 ice cubes into it (to create steam) and bake the dough for approximately 20–25 minutes. Brush the surface with melted butter immediately after removing the loaf from the oven.

Note: if you want to make wholewheat bread, simply use 150g white strong bread flour and 150g wholemeal flour and proceed as normal.

levain (natural sourdough starter or wild yeast)

Building a good levain or sourdough starter is a 10-day process, but it is worth it to be able to make a classic pain au levain at home. The bubbly, yeasty, batter-like levain will give your bread a moist open texture, fermented nutty sour flavour and an appealing red crust that is really satisfying.

You can make a rye pain au levain by replacing the strong bread flour with rye flour throughout this recipe, but the resulting dough will be stiffer because rye flour absorbs more moisture.

Day One
400g strong bread flour
500ml water at about 25°C
Mix the flour and water together to a smooth batter in a large bowl, preferably glass.
Cover the bowl with muslin and place the bowl somewhere outside out of direct sunlight
but where it will get plenty of fresh air.

Day Two
Hopefully, some bubbles have appeared on the surface after 24 hours. Using a wooden
spoon, beat air into the mixture, and replace muslin cover. Leave for another 24 hours.

Days Three and Four
There should be quite a few bubbles appearing on the surface. To encourage more, feed
the levain.
Add:
200ml water at about 25°C
200g strong bread flour
Pour the water in first and break up the culture in the water, then add the flour and mix well.
Cover the bowl with the muslin again and let it stand in a warm place. Leave for 24 hours
before feeding it again with the same quantities of flour and water.

Days Five and Six
As the wild yeast spores multiply, they start getting through their food a bit quicker, so you
need to feed them more regularly. About 12 hours after the last feeding on Day Four, you
need to pour off half of the culture, and feed the remainder with the same quantities of flour
and water as on Day Three and Day Four. Twelve hours later, feed the culture again.

Day Seven and Beyond
Having captured wild yeasts, you now need to keep them alive — having a levain becomes
a bit like owning a pet. Yeast needs to be fed three times a day if it is to perform well.

First Feed
100g starter (discard the rest)
40g strong bread flour
60ml water at about 25°C
Allow to ferment for about 8 hours.

Second Feed
200g starter
80g strong bread flour
120ml water at about 25°C
Allow to ferment for about 8 hours.

Third Feed
400g starter
160g strong bread flour
240ml water at about 25°C
Allow to ferment for 8 hours.

After a couple of weeks, if all has gone well, you should have a happy and healthy sourdough starter living in your home, as a new member of the family. From about Day 10 it will be strong enough to make bread, and its strength will increase as it matures. Over time, it will develop consistency, balance and, to a certain extent, immunity from foreign invaders.

The Feeding Schedule

The timing of your feeding schedule can be organised to suit your day, and your baking plans. I prefer to make my dough first thing in the morning, so my feeding schedule looks something like this:
8am the day before baking, first feed
8pm the day before baking, second feed
8am baking day, make your dough

If you are just maintaining your starter but not planning to make bread, throwing out nearly a kilo of starter every day may seem quite wasteful – and it is. Once your starter is bubbling along in a healthy way (at least two weeks after Day One), you can store it in the fridge while you are not using it. If you want to do this, it should be done just after the first feed, so the yeast has some food for its hibernation. In the fridge most of the wild yeasts will go dormant. As time goes on, though, these dormant spores will start to die off. So while the starter is in cold storage, it will still need the occasional feed. This can be done once a week, with the same amounts as for normal feeding (discarding the excess as required), but with slightly warmer water (about 35°C). This will allow the yeasts to feed for a while before going dormant in the cold again. A word of warning: you will need to get the starter back on two to three feeds a day at room temperature at least two days before you bake with it. If you try to make bread with starter straight from the fridge you will fail.

Feeding Amounts

The amount of water and flour fed to a sourdough starter once it is healthy varies from baker to baker. The feeding amounts below are a good guide. The amount of healthy sourdough starter can vary, but the formula should stay the same. Total weight of sourdough starter should be fed with half its amount of water and half its amount of flour.

Example:
250 g healthy sourdough starter
125 ml water
125 g flour
_____

500 g new sourdough starter

sweet pastry

170g butter, softened
85g sugar
1 small egg

260g plain flour, sifted
4 drops vanilla essence
zest of ½ lemon

Using a wooden spoon, beat the butter and sugar together until light and creamy. Add the egg and mix until combined. Lastly add the flour, vanilla and lemon zest and mix until the dough comes away from the sides of the bowl. Wrap in plastic wrap and refrigerate for 30 minutes or, even better, overnight.

butter puff pastry

300g strong bread flour
50g chilled butter
good pinch of salt

150ml ice cold water
1 teaspoon fresh lemon juice
225g chilled butter for layering

Rub the flour, chilled butter and salt between your fingers to form a coarse crumb. Add the ice cold water and lemon juice and mix to form a firm dough. Tip the dough out onto a lightly floured bench and knead for 2–3 minutes and form into a ball. Cover the dough with plastic wrap and allow to rest for 5–10 minutes. Using a rolling pin, and on a lightly floured bench, roll out the dough to a 1cm-thick 25cm square.

Ensure the layering butter is the same consistency as the dough and place it in a single layer inside the rolled out square of dough. Fold each corner of the dough into the centre to encase the layering butter in an envelope, obtaining two layers of dough and one layer of layering fat.

Now give the pastry four 'single turns':

· Roll out the pastry to a 1cm thick rectangle. Divide the rectangle into thirds.

· Fold A to C and then D to B, making three layers of pastry.

· Cover the pastry with plastic wrap to prevent drying out and skinning. Rest for 15–20 minutes.

· Repeat this process three more times allowing 20–30 minutes rest between each turn.

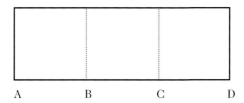

A   B   C   D

The pastry is now ready to be used, but it can be covered and stored in the refrigerator for up to 3 days or in the freezer for 3 months.

1. Rolling and folding to achieve a half fold.

Points to consider when processing puff pastry:

· Ensure that all your ingredients are kept cool.
· Always ensure that your dough and layering fat are the same consistency when incorporating the layering fat.
  Always use chilled water. In the summer you need to use iced chilled water (but do not put the ice cubes in the dough, as they will not dissolve during mixing).
· When rolling and folding your puff pastry, use as little dusting flour as possible and brush away any excess flour before completing each fold.
· Always keep your bench lightly floured during the rolling out process. Never allow the pastry to stick to the bench.
· When rolling out for each fold, ensure that the open ends are folded back into the centre of the dough.
· Always keep to the resting times stated to avoid shrinkage in the finished baked product.
· When rolling and folding your puff pastry, use as little dusting flour as possible and brush away any excess flour before completing each fold.
  Always keep your bench lightly floured during the rolling out process. Never allow the pastry to stick to the bench.
· When rolling out for each fold, ensure that the open ends are folded back into the centre of the dough.
· Always keep to the resting times stated to avoid shrinkage in the finished baked product.
· During resting periods keep the pastry covered with plastic wrap and keep it cool in the refrigerator.
· Always rest your puff pastry products before baking – the longer the better (anywhere from 2–12 hours in the refrigerator). Allow to warm to room temperature before placing in the oven.

How does puff pastry rise?

Once the hundreds of layers of dough and layering fat begin to heat up in the oven (the oven must be at the correct temperature when the pastry is put in), the fat melts and the moisture within the dough begins to produce steam. The protein (gluten) in the dough layers begins to expand and separate. The steam pushes the dough layers upwards.

Once the puff pastry has reached its maximum volume and all the moisture within the dough has escaped, the protein (gluten) begins to coagulate (set), giving it its structure.

If the puff pastry is taken out of the oven before coagulation (setting) is complete the structure will collapse.

black sesame seed short pastry

160g standard plain flour
2 tablespoons black sesame seeds
120g butter
good pinch of salt
50ml cold water

Place the flour, sesame seeds, butter and salt into a large mixing bowl and use your fingertips to gently rub the ingredients together until they resemble rough bread crumbs. Do not overmix or the butter will begin to melt from the heat of your fingers.

Add the water and mix until a dough is formed. Cover with plastic wrap and refrigerate for 30 minutes or overnight.

Before using, gently rework the pastry, taking care to ensure it remains cold and firm. Roll it out on a lightly floured workbench, into a sheet about 3mm thick or as stated in your recipe.

basic sponge cake

4 eggs, warmed
125g caster sugar
125g plain flour
50g melted butter

a few drops of vanilla essence (optional)
butter for greasing
flour for coating

Put the warmed eggs and sugar in the bowl of an electric mixer fitted with a whisk and whisk together to the ribbon stage — the mixture will be thick and when trailed on itself it will hold its own weight for about 10 seconds.

Sift the flour and carefully fold through the foamy liquid. Once the flour is three-quarters incorporated into the egg and sugar foam, add the melted butter and vanilla, if using, and continue to fold through gently. Avoid over-mixing at this stage to avoid losing the air bubbles you have created.

Immediately pour the mixture into a 20cm round cake tin that has been greased with butter and coated with flour. Bake for 25–30 minutes in a preheated oven set at 190°C until the sponge is set.

ingredients

wheat flour

Wheat flour is the most important ingredient in the bakery. It provides bulk and structure to most of the baker's products, including breads, cakes, biscuits and pastries. It's important to understand that there are many different types of flour and each has been developed with a particular bakery product in mind.

Flour is obtained from the cereal wheat. A grain of wheat consists of six main parts, but for baking, the endosperm, bran and the germ are the most important.

The endosperm (85 per cent) is the white part of the wheat grain, from which white flour is milled once the bran and germ have been removed. It consists largely of:
· tightly packed starch granules,
· soluble proteins (albumens),
· insoluble gluten-forming proteins (glutenin and gliadin),
· oil,
· moisture, and
· mineral matter.

Bran (13 per cent) is the multi-layered outside skin of the wheat grain, which is removed during milling. It is an excellent source of dietary fibre and is blended back into finely ground endosperm (white flour) to produce wheatmeal or brown flour.

The germ (2 per cent) located inside the wheat grain and is the embryo from which wheat can reproduce itself. It is mostly removed in the milling of white flour because the oil it contains soon becomes rancid and the enzymes it produces have a detrimental influence on the fermentation process in bread-making. The germ is blended back into the endosperm and bran to produce wholemeal flour and is rich in:
· oil
· calcium
· vitamin B, and
· enzymes.

The composition of flour will naturally be similar to that of the wheat from which it is milled. An average composition would be as follows.

constituents	strong flour %	soft flour %
Starch	70	72
Insoluble gluten-forming proteins	13	8
Moisture	13–15	13–15
Sugar	2.5	2.5
fat	1–1.5	1–1.5
Soluble proteins	1	1
Mineral salts	0.5	0.5

The insoluble, gluten-forming proteins present in flour are known as gluten. Gluten is made up of two different proteins, glutenin and gliadin, which have different characteristics. Glutenin produces elastic properties and gliadin produces extensible properties. Gluten is produced in a bread dough for example, when water has been added and the dough has been mixed sufficiently to develop the gluten. The suitability of a flour for bakery products is determined by the quality of the gluten and, in some cases, the quantity it contains. Flour that contains good-quality (and a lot of) gluten is known as strong flour; flour that contains a lower-quality (and less) gluten is known as soft flour.

types of flour

A wide variety of flours are milled from wheat and other grains for use in baking. Here are the most common types of flour.

- Bread flour contains a high level of protein (gluten). It is also known as strong flour and is used to make bread and yeast-raised varieties and puff pastry. Heavy fruitcakes are sometimes made using strong flours.
- Standard plain flour is a medium-strength flour and is used to make short pastry products and baking powder-aerated goods, such as scones, light fruit cakes, muffins, biscuits and slices.
- Self-raising flour is a medium-strength flour that has been blended with baking powder, which makes up approximately 6 per cent of the volume. It is used for batters, scones, pikelets and cakes. It is useful when small amounts of baking powder are required. You can make your own self-raising flour as follows:

      50g (2 cups) standard plain flour
      15g (3 teaspoons) baking powder
      Sieve together at least seven times.

- Wholemeal flour is milled from the whole wheat grain and therefore contains the bran and germ. It is suitable for all bread and yeast-raised products, pastries, cakes and biscuits. Bran acts like tiny pieces of glass within an unbaked product cutting and damaging the gluten (protein) network that has been developed in order to give strength, structure and volume to the finished baked product. Recipes using wholemeal flour make allowances for this.
- Semolina flour is simply coarsely-ground endosperm (flour) and can be used for thickening pie fillings, dusting the baker's peel for ease of transferring breads onto the oven hearth and as an ingredient in crusty bread formulations.
- Rye flour is the third most popular flour after white flour and wholemeal flour. Although rye flour contains some flour proteins, these proteins do not form gluten. Therefore, breads made with 100 per cent rye flour will be sticky at the dough stage and heavy and dense after baking. Rye breads are by far the most popular breads in Germany and Eastern Europe.
- Cornflour is also known as corn starch. It is obtained from the cereal maize. It is almost 100 per cent starch and does not contain any insoluble gluten-forming

proteins. Cornflour is mainly used as a thickening agent for custards, sauces and fillings.

- Rice flour is obtained from rice. It is almost 100 per cent starch and does not contain any insoluble gluten-forming proteins. Rice flour is added to cake recipes and biscuits to assist in absorption of liquids to improve keeping qualities or crispness. An example is in shortbread.
- Soya flour is obtained from the soya bean. It is very rich in protein, but does not contain any insoluble gluten-forming proteins. It is very high in fat, making it an excellent ingredient for any bread recipe that requires keeping qualities, even texture and increased volume.
- Malt flour and malt products are obtained from barley and wheat that have undergone a controlled process known as malting, which begins after the grains have been cleaned. Germination takes place in a temperature- and humidity-controlled environment. During this period, the starch within the grain is converted into simple sugars. This process is halted when the grains are heated during the drying stages of the process. Malt is an important food source for yeast in yeasted dough.
- Cornmeal is also known as polenta and is made from kernels of corn or maize. Yellow cornmeal is made from whole kernels and is ground to a fine, medium or coarse texture.
- Organic flour is milled from organically-grown wheat — wheat that is grown by selected farmers and not contaminated by wheat that has been treated with chemical sprays, etc. Commercial flour mills are unable to process organic grains in conjunction with other grains. Organic flour is ground in mills dedicated for milling organic flour. All baked products can be made using organic flour. Quality is sometimes variable.
- Spelt flour is made from the spelt grain, which has been found by archaeologists in many prehistoric sites. Although it comes from the same family as wheat, it has a different genetic structure and is higher in protein, vitamins and minerals. Some people with wheat allergies may be able to tolerate spelt products. Today, it is grown commercially and makes marvellous bread with a rich, nutty flavour. It is a popular organic flour.

Many types of flour are also available in wholegrain or kibbled (cut) grain forms. They are are used when making wholegrain or multi-cereal breads, but the grains need soaking for at least 12 hours in equal quantities of water and grain in order to soften before use.

salt

Salt is a natural mineral found in many parts of the world. It comes in many different forms: table salt, sea salt, iodised salt, vacuum salt and rock salt. It is more than just a flavour or seasoning enhancer as it also strengthens the gluten structure and makes it more stretchable. It controls the rate of fermentation within yeast-raised doughs, enhancing the flavour and eating qualities. Salt is hygroscopic and should be stored away from moisture.

sugar

Sugar, or sucrose, is obtained from two sources: sugar cane and sugar beet. Both are natural substances and belong to the chemical group of carbohydrates. Once the refining of sugar has been completed it can be categorised in two divisions: grains and syrups.

eggs

Eggs are used in large quantities within the bakery and are more expensive than many of the other ingredients used. A whole egg consists of a yolk, a white and a shell. The size of the egg can affect the final product from a recipe so it is often necessary to weigh eggs after they have been tipped from the shell.

milk

Whole milk is fresh milk as it comes from the cow, with nothing added or removed. It contains 3.5 per cent fat (known as milk fat), 8.5 per cent non-fat milk solids and 88 per cent water. Fresh milk should always be kept in the refrigerator and the use-by date adhered to. Milk is also processed into different forms, such as milk powders, condensed milk and evaporated milk.

fresh cream

Fresh cream is obtained from the fat content of cow's milk. Fresh cream is not often used as a liquid in doughs or batters, except in a few specialty products. Cream is more important in the production of fillings, toppings, dessert sauces and cold desserts such as mousses. If whipping fresh cream, care should be taken to avoid overwhipping. The only thing to do with overwhipped cream is to continue whipping it to produce butter. When whipped correctly, cream should double in volume.

butter

Butter is by far the most commonly used fat in baking. It has a low melting point and, therefore, melts very quickly in the baking process. Some recipes call for hard, softened or even melted butter and it is important to pay attention and use the correct type as it can affect quality of the final product.

baking powder

Baking powder is a mixture of an acid (cream of tartar) and an alkali (bicarbonate of soda). It is responsible for the aeration, final volume and, often, the crumb structure of a product. When baking powder becomes moist during the mixing process and heated in the oven, there is a reaction between the acid and alkali, which produces a gas (carbon dioxide). The gas lifts and pushes up the final product until the proteins from the eggs and flour have coagulated (set) during baking. All batters and doughs containing baking powder should be kept cool (21 °C or below) and prepared quickly to prevent the gas from forming before the mixture enters the oven.

nuts

All nuts have a limited shelf-life because of their high fat content and can turn rancid in a very short time if not stored correctly. All nuts should be kept in a cool place and, if purchased in large quantities, they should be stored in the freezer. Here are the most common types of nuts.

· Almonds are used whole with skins on, blanched, split, flaked, shelled, crushed or ground.
· Walnuts are used whole or as pieces for decoration and chopped for adding to doughs and batters.
· Pecans are generally used in premium goods, due to the cost.
· Peanuts are the only nut grown in the ground.
· Coconut is used in cakes and biscuits or as a coating or decoration.
· Hazelnuts have a distinctive sweet flavour and are best if lightly roasted before use.

fruits

Most fruit can be dried for later use. Currants, sultanas, raisins, mixed peel, figs, dates and apricots are most commonly available, but peaches, nectarines, apples and bananas are available, too. All are suitable to add to dough and batter mixtures and fillings. Preparation for use may involve washing, drying, cleaning, removing stones and stalks and soaking in water or alcohol to moisten the fruit. Fresh, tinned and frozen fruit and berries are all useful additions to baked products.

cocoa

Cocoa is the dry powder that remains after part of the cocoa butter is removed from chocolate liquor. Cocoa contains starch, which tends to absorb moisture in a cake batter, so when using cocoa powder use less flour to keep the recipe balanced. Dutch cocoa powder is further processed to neutralise the natural acidity of cocoa.

couverture

Couverture is a type of chocolate prepared by milling cocoa butter, cocoa and sugar together. It is expensive and is usually used to make top-quality, high-class chocolate products. Couverture needs tempering before use. Tempering is a heating and cooling process that ensures the couverture sets. To temper couverture follow the steps set out below:

Step 1   Half fill a saucepan with cold water, bring to the boil, turn off the heat and remove the saucepan from the heat.

Step 2   Break the chocolate into small pieces and place in a stainless steel bowl that will fit inside the saucepan of water. Place the bowl of chocolate in the hot water. Never allow any water to come in contact with the chocolate as this will cause the chocolate to thicken.

Step 3   Stir the chocolate with a clean wooden spoon until it has reached 40°C and the chocolate has melted. You may need to remove the bowl from the water from time to time to avoid overheating the chocolate.

Step 4   Tip two-thirds of the chocolate on to a marble slab or cold clean work surface and using two palette knives rotate the chocolate until the chocolate has cooled to a temperature if of 27°C.

Step 5   Place the cooled chocolate with the other one-third and mix thoroughly until well combined.

Step 6   Place the bowl back over the warm water and warm the couverture to exactly 30°C. Always use at this temperature and you will achieve a nice sheen on the chocolate once it has set.

Chocolate compound — known as chocolate coating — is prepared from vegetable fats, cocoa powder, sugar, milk solids and emulsifiers. It is much easier to use than couverture and does not require any special preparation. Melt by following steps 1–3 above. It is available in dark, milk and white chocolate.

Caution: do not allow water or steam to come into contact with any chocolate because the chocolate will thicken and become unusable.

spices

Spices are aromatic agents used to flavour food that are obtained from the buds, seeds, flowers, fruit, leaves, roots, stems and bark of certain plants. Spices are used whole or ground, but the ground form loses its flavour rapidly. Replace spices after six months. Spices should be used in moderation in baked goods.

yeast

Yeast is a living single-cell organism that can only be seen under a microscope. The strain used by commercial bakers is called *Saccharomyces cerevisiae*. Yeast is responsible for the volume in bread, buns, rolls, croissants, Danish pastries and similar products. The activity of yeast in dough is called fermentation. That's the process by which yeast acts on sugars and changes them into carbon dioxide and alcohol. The release of gas produces the rising action — also known as leavening —in yeast-raised products. The alcohol evaporates completely during and immediately after baking.

In order for yeast to produce carbon dioxide and alcohol, four conditions are required: time, moisture, warmth (ideally between 28–32°C), and food. Without these conditions the yeast will die and cause an inferior product.

Fresh yeast or compressed yeast can be purchased from selected supermarkets and delicatessens. It has a limited shelf-life and cannot be frozen.

Instant active dried yeast can be purchased from most supermarkets. It has an excellent shelf-life if unopened. When using instant active dried yeast in place of fresh yeast, use one-third less; for example, if a recipe requires 15 grams of fresh yeast, use 5 grams of instant active dried yeast.

There are many types of dried yeast, which can cause confusion, but instant active dried yeast does not need to be added to water before use. Simply add it to the flour and mix through.

water

In bread doughs, warm water (20–25°C) is usually used but, sometimes, chilled water is called for to control the speed of fermentation of the dough.

basic savoury recipes

anchovy dressing

8–10 anchovy fillets (to taste)
1 clove garlic, diced
cracked pepper
1 egg yolk
1 cup olive oil
juice of 1 lemon

Put anchovy, garlic and a good grind of pepper in a food processor and blend to form a paste. Add the egg yolk and blend. With the motor running on low, very slowly pour the oil through the feeder tube and continue blending until a smooth mayonnaise has formed. Add the lemon juice and blend to combine. Cover and refrigerate until required.

asian marinade for duck or lamb

This makes enough for 1 kg of meat.

juice of 1 lemon
2 tablespoons fish sauce
2 tablespoons sesame oil
1 clove garlic, finely diced
salt and pepper

Mix all ingredients together until combined. Cover and refrigerate until required.

basic chermoula paste for fish & vegetables

1 cup parsley
2 cups coriander leaves
2 cloves garlic, roughly diced
1½ teaspoons ground turmeric
1 teaspoon ground cumin
juice and rind of 1 lemon
1–1½ cups grapeseed oil

Put the parsley, coriander, garlic, turmeric and cumin in a food processor and blend to form a smooth paste. Add lemon juice and rind and blend to combine. With the motor running on low, very slowly pour the oil through the feeder tube and continue blending to form a smooth paste.

basic tomato sauce for pasta or pizza

4 cloves garlic, finely diced
4 tablespoons olive oil
4 anchovy fillets
2 x 400g tins whole peeled tomatoes, hand crushed
½ teaspoon dried wild Italian oregano
½ cup dry white wine
salt and pepper

Sauté the garlic in the oil until aromatic. Add anchovies and stir to combine. Add tomatoes, oregano and wine and bring to the boil. Simmer, uncovered, stirring occasionally — 20 minutes for pasta sauce and 25–30 minutes for pizza sauce.

brandade dip

150g cod fillets, skinned and
    bones removed
200g rock salt
1 small potato
200ml milk
1 sprig thyme
2 cloves of garlic, peeled
20g olive oil
salt and pepper to taste

Rub the cod fillets with the rock salt,
coating both sides. Cover and leave
overnight in the refrigerator. The next day,
remove the cod from the refrigerator, rinse
with cold water and soak in cold water for
8–12 hours to fully remove the salt.

Peel and dice the potato, place it into a
saucepan with the milk, thyme and garlic
and bring to the boil.

Add the drained cod fillets and poach
until the potato and cod are cooked.
Remove the thyme sprig and place the
cod, potato and garlic in a food processor,
reserving the milk. Blend until a smooth
purée is formed.

Slowly add the milk until the mixture
just holds its shape (the mixture will
thicken slightly when standing). Add the
olive oil and blend in. Season with salt and
freshly ground pepper to taste. Remove
from the blender and place into serving
bowls, cover and chill in the refrigerator
until required.

curry powder for vegetable curry

2 tablespoons cumin seeds
$\frac{1}{2}$ teaspoon cardamom seeds
$\frac{1}{2}$ teaspoon fenugreek seeds
$\frac{1}{2}$ teaspoon coriander seed
$\frac{1}{2}$ teaspoon ground nutmeg
1 teaspoon black peppercorns

Toast the cumin, cardamom, fenugreek
and coriander seeds. Transfer to a mortar
and pestle and add the nutmeg and peppercorns. Grind together to a powder and store
in an airtight container until required.

double soy vinaigrette

75ml Japanese light soy
50ml Chinese dark soy
100ml Chinese rice wine vinegar
2 cloves garlic, finely diced

Mix all ingredients together until
combined. Cover and store in the
refrigerator until required.

tarragon sherry vinaigrette

2 tablespoons chopped fresh tarragon
60ml sherry vinegar
1 clove garlic, finely diced
100ml olive oil
salt and pepper

Mix all ingredients together until combined.
Season to taste with salt and pepper. Cover
and store in the refrigerator until required.

eggplant dip

1 large or 2 medium eggplants
2 garlic cloves, crushed
2 tablespoon tahini (sesame paste)
$\frac{1}{4}$ cup scallions, finely chopped
juice of 1 lemon
$\frac{1}{4}$ cup chopped parsley
ground paprika

Preheat oven to 200°C. Prick eggplant all over with a fork and place on an oven tray in oven for 45–50 minutes until very soft. Remove from oven, plunge in cold water to cool or simply wait for the eggplant to cool.

Peel and chop cooked eggplant, then place in a blender with the garlic, tahini, scallions, lemon juice and parsley. Blend until almost smooth. Place into a small bowl and refrigerate until ready to serve. Just before serving, sprinkle a little paprika on top.

Makes about 2 cups.

kaffir lime & ginger syrup for grilled fruit & pork

1cm piece root ginger, peeled
   and shredded
4 large kaffir lime leaves, spines
   removed, finely shredded
$\frac{1}{2}$ cup cold water
$\frac{1}{2}$ cup sugar
juice of 2 large limes

Put all ingredients in a heavy-based saucepan and bring to the boil. Reduce the heat and simmer for 4–6 minutes until the mixture thickens. Cover and store in the refrigerator until required.

laksa paste

4 cloves garlic
2cm piece root ginger, peeled
6 spring onions
1 stalk lemongrass, bashed and sliced
1 red chilli (or more to taste)
2 tablespoons fish sauce

Put all ingredients in a food processor or mortar and pestle and grind together. Add just enough water to form a smooth paste. Cover and store in the refrigerator until required.

lemon dressing

115ml olive oil
$2\frac{1}{2}$ tablespoons lemon juice
$\frac{1}{2}$ teaspoon French mustard
sea salt and freshly ground pepper

Mix together and store in an airtight container until required.

mayonnaise

3 egg yolks
juice of $\frac{1}{2}$ lemon
1 cup olive oil
salt and pepper

Put egg yolks and lemon juice in a food processor and blend until combined. With the motor running on low, very slowly pour the oil through the feeder tube and continue blending until a smooth mayonnaise has formed. Season to taste with salt and pepper.

mediterranean marinade for fish or lamb

This makes enough for 1 kg of meat.

1 teaspoon finely chopped rosemary
1 clove garlic, finely diced
6 tablespoons olive oil
6 tablespoons raspberry vinegar
salt and pepper

Mix all ingredients together until combined. Cover and store in the refrigerator until required.

nahm jim dressing

This is ideal for for Asian salads or as a dipping sauce.

3 red chillies, deseeded
2 bird's-eye chillies, deseeded
4 garlic cloves
4 coriander roots, cleaned
3 tablespoons grated palm sugar
3 tablespoons fish sauce
juice of 8 limes

Grind the chillies, garlic, and coriander root into a paste in a mortar and pestle. Add the sugar and the fish sauce and grind until well combined. Transfer to a bowl and stir in the lime juice.

north african marinade for grilled vegetables or pork

This makes enough for 1 kg of meat.

1 tablespoon Spanish smoked paprika
juice of 2 lemons
1 clove garlic, finely diced
2 teaspoons ground coriander
salt and pepper

Mix all ingredients together until combined. Cover and store in the refrigerator until required.

olive, sun-dried tomato & cashew tapenade

200g kalamata black olives, drained and pitted
125g tuna in oil, drained
20g fresh basil, washed and dried
4 anchovy fillets, drained
1 garlic clove, crushed
zest of 1 lemon
2 tablespoons of lemon juice
ground black pepper
good pinch salt
50g sun-dried tomatoes
50g cashew nuts
2 tablespoons extra virgin olive oil
salt and pepper to taste

Place all the ingredients except the olive oil and salt and pepper into a food processor and blend until a rough texture is formed, then slowly pour the olive oil through the opening while the food processor is working. Take care not to make the tapenade too smooth — it should be rough in texture so you can see elements of the ingredients. Season with salt and pepper. Place into an airtight container and store for up to 2 weeks. This mixture is enough for 2 batches.

onion jam

2 medium onions, peeled and
   thinly sliced
1 bay leaf
1 sprig fresh rosemary
1 tablespoon olive oil
1 tablespoon balsamic vinegar
25g brown sugar
$\frac{1}{2}$ tablespoon yellow mustard seeds
$\frac{1}{2}$ tablespoon black mustard seeds

Sauté the onions, bay leaf and rosemary in olive oil until well browned. Add the vinegar and stir well to deglaze the pan. Add the sugar and mustard seeds, cover and cook on a low heat for 30 minutes. Check to make sure the mixture does not dry out and add a drop or two of water, if necessary — the onion jam should be quite thick and a shiny rich brown colour. Cool and store in an airtight container in the refrigerator until required.

pesto verde

100g fresh basil
15g pine nuts, toasted
25g freshly grated Parmesan
   cheese
75ml extra virgin olive oil
salt and pepper

Process the basil, pine nuts, Parmesan and a little olive oil and with the motor running,

add more olive oil in a steady stream until the sauce has reached desired consistency. Season to taste with salt and pepper.

pizza base

This can be broken down into balls and frozen until required.

15g dried yeast
6 tablespoons lukewarm water
3 tablespoons OO Italian flour
   or plain flour
2 $\frac{1}{2}$ cups extra flour
pinch of salt
$\frac{3}{4}$ cup extra lukewarm water

Put the yeast and first measures of water and flour in a bowl large enough to allow them to double in size. Mix to form a soup. Cover with a damp towel or plastic wrap and set aside in a warm, draught-free place for 30 minutes or until doubled in size

Place the remaining flour and salt into a large bowl and add the soup mixture and combine. Add extra water as required to form a dough mass. Form dough into a ball and remove from the bowl. Tip onto a lightly floured bench and knead on a floured surface for 10 minutes until shiny and elastic. Place back into the bowl, cover and stand in a warm draught-free place for another 30 minutes.

preserved tomatoes

1.5kg Roma tomatoes
6 cloves garlic, lightly crushed
handful of basil leaves
handful of fresh oregano
handful of bay leaves

Pack the tomatoes into sterilised jars,
layering with the garlic and herbs.
Remove any air bubbles and seal the jars.

Stand the sealed jars upright in a
saucepan and cover with boiling water.
Bring the water to the boil and continue
to boil for 30 minutes. Remove from the
heat and allow to cool completely before
removing the jars from the saucepan.

Check that the jars have sealed
correctly. Stored in a cool dark pantry,
these will keep for several months.

roasted field mushrooms

12 large portabello mushrooms
2 cloves garlic, finely diced
2 tablespoon balsamic vinegar
4 sage leaves
leaves from 1 large sprig of rosemary
   pulled from the stalk
$\frac{1}{2}$ cup olive oil
sprigs of thyme
sea salt

Arrange the mushrooms in a single layer
on a baking tray. Mix all other ingredients
together and liberally brush over the
mushrooms. Sprinkle with sea salt. Bake
in a preheated oven set at 160°C for 20–25
minutes.

roasted garlic aïoli

3 egg yolks
1–2 heads roasted garlic (to taste)
   (see page 99)
$1\frac{1}{2}$ cups olive oil
salt and pepper

Put egg yolks and garlic in a food
processor and blend until combined.
With the motor running on low, very
slowly pour the oil through the feeder
tube and continue blending until a
smooth mayonnaise has formed.
Season to taste with salt and pepper.

simple thai curry paste

1 onion, diced
1 lemongrass stalk, very finely chopped
2cm piece galangal, finely chopped
4 cloves garlic
1–2 chillies (to taste)
2 coriander roots, cleaned and finely
   chopped
2 tablespoons curry paste

Put all ingredients in a food processor or
mortar and pestle and grind together. Add
just enough water to form a smooth paste.
Cover and refrigerate until required.

slow-roasted tomatoes

2 stems vine-ripened tomatoes
2 cloves garlic, finely diced
2 teaspoons finely chopped rosemary
$1/3$ cup olive oil
1 tablespoon olive oil
salt and pepper

Place the tomatoes on a baking tray. Mix all other ingredients together and liberally brush over the tomatoes. Bake in a pre-heated oven set at 120°C for 1–1 $1/4$ hours.

sun-dried tomato pesto

1 cup sun-dried tomatoes in oil
$1/2$ cup tightly packed basil leaves
$1/2$ cup whole almonds, toasted
4 cloves garlic
1 teaspoon lemon zest
$1/4$ teaspoon coarse salt
$1/4$ cup grated Parmesan cheese
1 cup olive oil

Drain, rinse, and pat dry the sun-dried tomatoes. In a large food processor process the basil, toasted almonds, garlic, lemon zest, and salt. Process until coarsely chopped. Add the tomatoes and cheese and process until the tomatoes are coarsely chopped. With the motor running, add the olive oil in a steady stream and process until the pesto comes together. Store in an airtight container in the refrigerator for up to 6 weeks.

thai sweet chilli sauce

200g sugar
$1 1/4$ cups rice wine vinegar
3–4 chillies, deseeded and finely
   chopped (to taste)
4 cloves garlic, finely diced

Heat sugar and vinegar to boiling, stirring until the sugar has dissolved. Add chillies and garlic, reduce heat and simmer for 10 minutes. Allow to cool before using. If not using immediately, cover and store in the refrigerator until required.

wasabi & vietnamese mint dressing

2 tablespoons wasabi paste
juice of 1 lime
8 leaves Vietnamese mint, chopped
2 tablespoons palm sugar, grated
3 tablespoons Chinese rice wine vinegar

Combine all ingredients and stir until the sugar has dissolved. Cover and store in the refrigerator until required.

wheat-free baking powder

60g sodium bicarbonate
130g cream of tartar
60g non-wheat flour

Mix all the ingredients together and sift through a fine sieve. Store in a dry, airtight container until required.

basic sweet recipes

apricot glaze

300g apricot jam
150g water

Bring apricot jam and water to the boil. Strain through a fine sieve and use hot. You may need to warm the glaze from time to time.

balsamic reduction

350ml balsamic vinegar
1 tablespoon brown sugar
1 star anise
$\frac{1}{2}$ cinnamon stick

Bring all ingredients to a simmer on a low heat for 1 hours until reduced by two thirds — it will be thick and syrupy. Strain through a fine sieve and remove the star anise and cinnamon stick. Cool and put into a squirty bottle, store in the refrigerator but use at room temperature. It will keep for a long time.

basil syrup

$\frac{1}{2}$ cup fresh basil leaves
$\frac{1}{4}$ cup spinach leaves
$\frac{1}{4}$ cup of simple sugar syrup
   (see page 244)

Blanch the basil and spinach in boiling water for 10 seconds. Refresh in iced water, drain and squeeze to remove excess water. Pureé in a blender with sugar syrup for 3 minutes or until bright green. Strain through a very fine sieve. Store in the refrigerator until required.

calvados apple purée

2 Granny Smith apples
50 ml water
100ml Calvados liqueur

Peel, core and dice the apples. Bring the apples and water to the boil with the lid on. Reduce the heat to a simmer and cook until the apples are completely soft — stir occasionally to avoid the apples from colouring and burning. Add the Calvados and cook for a further 2 minutes. Remove from the heat and purée using a stick blender until smooth. Pass through a fine sieve and set aside to cool. Store in the refrigerator until required.

caramel sauce

50ml water
60g sugar
150ml cream

Boil water and sugar until golden in colour. Remove from heat and stir in the cream. Return to the heat and simmer for 5 minutes or until thick.

crème chantilly

200ml fresh cream
25g fine sugar
seeds scraped from 1 vanilla pod

Whisk the cream, sugar and vanilla seeds together until soft or stiff peaks form, depending on the use. Cover and refrigerate until required — you may need to re-whip it a little before serving to achieve the desired consistency.

crunchy praline

100g sugar
squeeze of lemon juice
100g almond flakes, lightly toasted

Put the sugar and lemon juice in a heavy-based frying pan and cook until a golden caramel colour. Add the toasted almond flakes and immediately tip onto a lightly oiled bench. Allow to cool. Using a rolling pin, crush into small pieces. Store in an airtight container until required.

gin jelly cubes

3 sheets leaf gelatine
180g water
60g sugar
100ml gin

Soak the gelatine in a bowl of cold water to soften. Bring the water and sugar to the boil and remove from the heat. Squeeze the gelatine leaves to remove excess liquid and add to the hot syrup. Stir to dissolve. Set aside to cool then add the gin and pour into a slice tin, or other large shallow dish, lined with plastic wrap. The depth of the liquid should be no more than ¾ cm. Place in the refrigerator to set and cut into small cubes as required.

lemon curd

120g sugar
juice and zest of 2 medium-sized juicy lemons
4 egg yolks
60g butter

Whisk the sugar, lemon juice and zest and egg yolks together until combined — do not whip too much air into the mixture. Set over a saucepan of simmering water and gently whisk until the mixture thickens. After 10 minutes add the butter and continue to whisk for 5 minutes or until the butter has melted. Make sure the mixture does not get too hot otherwise the eggs will scramble. Once the lemon curd has thickened, cover with plastic wrap and set aside to cool. Refrigerate until required.

orange tuiles

100g sugar
100ml water
rind of 1 orange, julienned
75g plain flour
75g icing sugar
75g egg whites
75g melted butter

Dissolve the sugar in the water and poach the strips of rind over low heat until soft. Drain and dry with a paper towel. Set aside until required.

Sift the flour and icing sugar together. Using a wooden spoon stir in the egg whites and mix well. Add the melted butter and mix to form a smooth paste. Scrape down the bowl and cover with plastic wrap and rest the paste for 1 hour.

Cut a stencil out of a flat piece of

1–2mm thick plastic — I use a 6cm circle, but you can cut any shape you want.

Place the stencil onto a baking tray lined with non-stick baking paper and place a spoonful of tuile paste in the centre. Using a palette knife, spread the paste to the edges of the stencil. Peel off the stencil and place a few strips of candied orange strips on the top. Repeat until all the tuile paste has been used.

Bake for 5–10 minutes in a preheated oven set at 180°C until the edges have coloured but the middle remains pale. Using a palette knife, quickly lift the baked tuiles and shape them over a thin rolling pin or any other shape you want them to set into. Store in an airtight container until required.

For a change, you may like to sprinkle slivered almonds or poppyseeds on top instead of the candied peel.

pomegranate syrup

This is great with pancakes or ice cream or both.

seeds and juice from 2 whole pomegranates
1 ¼ cups cold water
½ cup sugar

Put all ingredients in a heavy-based saucepan and bring to the boil. Reduce the heat and simmer for 4–6 minutes until the mixture thickens. Cover and store in the refrigerator until required.

raspberry coulis

220g fresh or frozen raspberries
50g sugar or to taste
lemon juice to taste

Bring the raspberries to the boil, add sugar and stir to dissolve. Put into a blender and purée. Strain through a very fine sieve to remove any remaining seeds and adjust the tartness by adding lemon juice to taste. Cool and store in the refrigerator until required.

simple sugar syrup

200g sugar
200ml water

Heat sugar and water, stirring until sugar is dissolved. Bring to the boil, remove from heat and set aside to cool. Place in an airtight container and store in the refrigerator until required.

toffee sauce

250g sugar
50ml water
1 tablespoon butter
190ml cream

Bring the water and sugar to the boil in a heavy-based saucepan and cook until a golden caramel colour — 140°C on a sugar thermometer. Bring the cream to the boil. Remove both from the heat and stir to combine. Return to the heat and simmer for 5 minutes or until thick, stirring to ensure it is lump free. Add the butter and stir. Strain into an airtight container and store at room temperature until required.

vanilla ice cream

250ml cream
60ml milk
1 vanilla pod, split lengthways
2 egg yolks
$\frac{1}{3}$ cup sugar
1 tablespoon liquid glucose

Bring the cream, milk and vanilla pod to the boil, remove from the heat. Whisk the egg yolks and sugar together and pour in some of the hot cream and whisk to combine. Add the yolk mixture to the rest of the milk and cook for 2–3 minutes on a low heat until the mixture thickens slightly — it should coat the back of a spoon. Stir in the glucose and remove the vanilla pod. Strain through a fine sieve and cool. Place into an ice cream machine freeze and process according to manufacturer's instructions.

To make chocolate chip ice cream, add 250g finely chopped chocolate or chocolate chips to the strained custard.

white icing

1 cup icing sugar
$\frac{1}{4}$ teaspoon softened butter
zest of 1 lemon
1 tablespoon hot water (more or less)

Sift icing sugar and add butter. Add a little water and mix, adding more water as necessary to desired consistency — for spreading, piping or drizzling.

weights & measures

Standard spoon and cup measurements used in the recipes in this book are:

1 teaspoon = 5ml
1 tablespoon = 15ml
1 cup = 250ml

(All measures are level unless otherwise stated).

oven temperature

	°C	°F	Regulo Gas
Very slow	120	250	1
Slow	150	300	2
Moderately slow	160	325	3
Moderate	180	350	4
Moderately hot	190/200	370/400	5/6
Hot	210/220	410/440	6/7
Very hot	230	450	8
Super hot	250/290	475/550	9/10

conversion charts

liquid & volume measures

Metric	Imperial	American
5ml	$\frac{1}{6}$ fl oz	1 teaspoon
10ml	$\frac{1}{3}$ fl oz	1 dessertspoon
15ml	$\frac{1}{2}$ fl oz	1 tablespoon
60ml	2 fl oz	4 tablespoons
85ml	2 $\frac{1}{2}$ fl oz	$\frac{1}{3}$ cup
90ml	3 fl oz	$\frac{3}{8}$ cup (6 tablespoons)
125ml	4 fl oz	$\frac{1}{2}$ cup
180ml	6 fl oz	$\frac{3}{4}$ cup
250ml	8 fl oz	1 cup
300ml	10 fl oz ($\frac{1}{2}$ pint)	1 $\frac{1}{4}$ cups
375ml	12 fl oz	1 $\frac{1}{2}$ cups
435ml	14 fl oz	1 $\frac{3}{4}$ cups
500ml	16 fl oz	2 cups
625ml	20 fl oz (1 pint)	2 $\frac{1}{2}$ cups
750ml	24 fl oz	3 cups
1 litre	32 fl oz	4 cups
1.25 litres	40 fl oz (2 pints)	5 cups
1.5 litres	48 fl oz	6 cups
2.5 litres	80 fl oz (4 pints)	10 cups

dry measures

Metric	Imperial
30 grams	1 ounce
45 grams	$1\frac{1}{2}$ ounces
55 grams	2 ounces
70 grams	$2\frac{1}{2}$ ounces
85 grams	3 ounces
100 grams	$3\frac{1}{2}$ ounces
110 grams	4 ounces
125 grams	$4\frac{1}{2}$ ounces
140 grams	5 ounces
280 grams	10 ounces
450 grams	16 ounces (1 pound)
500 grams	1 pound, $1\frac{1}{2}$ ounces
700 grams	$1\frac{1}{2}$ pounds
800 grams	$1\frac{3}{4}$ pounds
1 kilogram	2 pounds, 3 ounces
1.5 kilograms	3 pounds, $4\frac{1}{2}$ ounces
2 kilograms	4 pounds, 6 ounces

acknowledgments
— *from the cook*

With any project like this there is always a number of people to thank. First, teaming up with Dean has been a great concept — we have both had a lot of fun planning, cooking and baking together for this book. It has also been a pleasure to work with Aaron and I have learnt a lot from him about food styling and photography.

Sonya McKinnon, Head Chef at Zarbo, has offered invaluable support, helping me prepare the dishes ready for Aaron to photograph. I think she enjoyed the challenge of doing something a bit different. Donna North, who took the photographs for my previous books, helped with some of the food styling and was a great gofer zipping around Auckland finding props for the photoshoot.

Another huge thank you goes to the loyal customers who have supported Zarbo over the past 15 years for their encouragement to me to write these books. It is rewarding that so many of you tell me that you do actually cook from these books.

Random House has also, once again, been hugely supportive throughout the whole process.

Finally, the biggest thank you goes to Cushla, Felix and Olive. They have to put up with me taking over the kitchen at home to test my recipes. They are always prepared to taste the results and provide robust, although not always supportive, comment.

Mark McDonough

acknowledgments
— *from the baker*

As with all books, there are many people to thank. Photographer Aaron McLean is at the top of my list — we call him 'the magician' and it is a real pleasure to work with him. You can find out more about his work at www.aaronmclean.com.

Thank you to Margaret Sinclair, Nicola Legat and the rest of the team at Random House New Zealand. As always, it's great to work with a talented team of professionals who give us total confidence.

Thank you to the team at my micro bakery Global Baker at Zarbo in Auckland: Olaf the head baker and Harish; Sonya the head chef, Caroline and Eric. Thanks also to the rest of the Zarbo team.

Also, thanks to the team at Baker & Spice in Shanghai: John, Jackie, David, Herman and the rest of the team. Without you all I could not be the Global Baker I have become. Keep up the passion, hard work, enthusiasm dedication and fun!

Paul Howley at Goodman Fielder/Champion Flour was there on hand to support us and we are very grateful.

To Julie Christie, Greg Heathcote and the team at EyeWorks, the Food TV channel and all the contestants of the first series of *Nestlé New Zealand's Hottest Home Baker* — thank you for helping me raise baking's profile by putting it on television.

Thank you to Air New Zealand. Mike Tod and his team brought me to New Zealand on numerous occasions and are great supporters of the Global Baker's expeditions.

To Tony Brown and his team at BAKEHOUSE in the United Kingdom, thank you for sharing my passion for baking.

Thanks to Donna North, Flotsam and Jetsam, Tid and Pieta Brenton, Japanese Lifestyle and Penelope Sinclair for the wonderful props used in the photography shoot.

Finally, thank you to my son Jason and my very supportive family, who are always there for me, and to all the people who have enjoyed my previous books. I am encouraged by the many emails and phone calls I receive — they make it all worthwhile.

Dean Brettschneider

AIR NEW ZEALAND

index

aioli: smoked sweet paprika aïoli 97
    roasted garlic aïoli 240
almond: almond cream filling 168
    almond frangipane fruit tartlets 198
    almond & rosemary biscotti 203
    almond & walnut tartlets 168
anchovy: anchovy dressing 235
    sun-dried tomato, black olive &
        anchovy dip 92
aniseed: fig & aniseed sourdough loaf 36
antipasti: sunflower & paprika rolls
    served with antipasti 16–18
apple: calvados apple purée 242
    fresh chunky apple, hazelnut, thyme
        & cabernet sauvignon rustico bread
        30–33
    plum & fennel tarte tatin with ice
        cream & apple purée 160
apricot glaze 242
asian lettuce cups 64
asian marinade 235
avocado: avocado, grapefruit salad with
    gazpacho dressing 78
    chilled avocado, lime & cucumber
        soup 80

bagel crisps 24
baguette: fig & aniseed sourdough loaf
    36
    global baker baguette traditional
        34–35
    moulding 215
balsamic reduction 166, 242
banana: dairy-free banana & walnut soya
    muffin 190
basic sponge cake 227
basic white or sandwich bread 221
basil: basil syrup 242
    beef carpaccio with basil caper purée
        84
    insalata caprese 77
    lemon cream mille-feuille with basil
        syrup 166
    pesto verde 239
    sun-dried tomato pesto 241
beans: greek-style baked cannellini beans
    with chicken balls 114
    mediterranean green bean salad 75

smoked fish, green bean & potato
    salad 134
winter vegetable soup with israeli
    couscous & borlotti beans 82
beef: asian lettuce cups 64
    beef carpaccio 84
    beef goulash 126
beetroot: beetroot, pumpkin, feta &
    roasted garlic focaccia-style quick
    bread 52
    beetroot, grilled lamb & haloumi salad
        144
belgian biscuits 207
berry stella healthy tart 196
biga ferment 30
biscotti, almond & rosemary 203
biscuit dough 207; see also cookies
black sesame seed see sesame seed
blue cheese: blue cheese & fig jam
    bruschetta topping 20
    chocolate & blue cheese tortellini 162
    traditional potted cheese 100
brandade dip 236
brandy snap 208
bread 12–56; see also buns, rolls
bread-making techniques 215–219
brie de meaux: whipped brie de meaux &
    crouton mille-feuille with rocket 23
bruschetta plate 20
buffalo mozzarella insalata caprese 77

cake: basic sponge cake 227
    danish dream cake 184
    devil's food chocolate cupcakes 186
    sticky stem-ginger cake 192
    sunken chocolate cake 170
cannellini beans: greek-style baked
    cannellini beans 114
capsicum: marinated chargrilled
    capsicums 99
caramel sauce 162, 242
cashew, olive & sun-dried tomato
    tapenade 238
cheese: savoury garden vegetable &
    cheese twist 46–47
    traditional potted cheese 100
chermoula paste for fish & vegetables
    235
chicken: chicken, bacon & corn soup 72
    chicken tenders 96

greek-style baked cannellini beans
    with chicken balls 114
roast poussin 128
salt brine for barbecued chicken 108
chilled avocado, lime & cucumber soup
    80
chilli: hot as hell sauce 131
    thai sweet chilli sauce 241
chocolate; see also chocolate, white
    chocolate & blue cheese tortellini on
        praline 162
    chocolate chip ice cream 245
    devil's food chocolate cupcakes 186
    ganache icing 186
    sunken chocolate cake 170
    triple chocolate chunk & pecan
        cookies 182
    tropical passionfruit & coconut
        chocolate truffles 204
chocolate, white
    ganache 195
    plum & fennel tarte tatin with white
        chocolate tuiles 160
    strawberries & cream truffles 206
    white chocolate chunk & cranberry
        chewy cookies 176
cinnamon & pecan easter quick bread
    twist 54
classic steamed mussels 138
coconut: danish dream cake 184
    tropical passionfruit & coconut
        chocolate truffles 204
cookies; see also biscotti
    belgian biscuits 207
    cranberry shortbread 180
    gingernut-stye cookies 178
    love heart jam dodgers 205
    triple chocolate chunk & pecan
        cookies 182
    white chocolate chunk & cranberry
        chewy cookies 176
corn: chicken, bacon & corn soup 72
couscous: israeli couscous, mango &
    pomegranate salad 106
    winter vegetable soup with israeli
        couscous 82
couverture 233
cranberry, dried: cranberry shortbread
    180
    fruit & nut loaf 41

white chocolate chunk & cranberry chewy cookies 176

cranberry juice: sour cherry & cranberry trifle 155–57

crème brûlée: espresso crème brûlée with nougatine spoon 164

crème chantilly 242–43

cucumber: chilled avocado, lime & cucumber soup 80
  pickled cucumber 68

curry: curry powder for vegetable curry 236
  green prawn curry 140
  simple thai curry paste 240

custard: sour cherry & cranberry trifle 155

dairy-free banana & walnut soya muffin 190

danish dream cake 184

dark devil's food chocolate cupcakes 186

dip: brandade 236
  eggplant 237
  goat's cheese, spinach & parsley 92
  sun-dried tomato, black olive & anchovy 92

dresdner christmas stollen 43–45

dressing: anchovy 235
  gazpacho 78
  horseradish 134
  lemon 20, 237
  mayonnaise 237
  nahm jim 238
  salad 150
  spicy peanut 149
  wasabi & vietnamese mint 241

duck: asian marinade for duck 235
  duck terrine 88

eggplant dip 237

espresso crème brûlée with nougatine spoon 164

fennel: plum & fennel tarte tatin 160

fermentation, bread dough
  bulk 215–16
  & salt 231
  & wheat germ 228
  yeast 234

feta: beetroot, pumpkin, feta & roasted garlic focaccia-style quick bread 52

fig & aniseed sourdough loaf 36

fish: italian fish stew 116
  smoked fish, green bean & potato salad 134

flour 228–30

focaccia: beetroot, pumpkin, feta & roasted garlic focaccia-style quick bread 52

frangipane: almond frangipane fruit tartlets 198

fresh chunky apple, hazelnut, thyme & cabernet sauvignon rustico bread 30–33

fruit, dried: fruit & nut loaf 39
  luxury milo fruit & nut slice 194

ganache icing 186, 195 (white)

garlic aïoli 240

gazpacho dressing 78

gin jelly cubes 166, 243

ginger: kaffir lime & ginger syrup 237
  sticky stem-ginger cake 192

gingernut-style cookies 178

global baker baguette traditional 34–35

goat's cheese: salami & rocket with lemon dressing & goat's cheese bruschetta 20
  goat's cheese, spinach & parsley dip 92

gorgonzola: poached peaches with prosciutto & gorgonzola 90

grapefruit: avocado, grapefruit salad with gazpacho dressing 78

greek-style baked cannellini beans with chicken balls 114

green prawn curry 140

grissini bread sticks 24

haloumi: beetroot, grilled lamb & haloumi salad 144

horseradish dressing 134

hot as hell sauce 131

hot cross buns 41–42

ice cream 160, 168, 245
  chocolate chip ice cream 245
  vanilla ice cream 245

icing see also ganache

lemon icing 192
  white icing 245

insalata caprese 77

israeli couscous, mango & pomegranate salad 106

italian blanched squid 71

italian fish stew 116

juniper: roast poussin with juniper, orange & black pepper 128

kaffir lime & ginger syrup for grilled fruit & pork 237

kneading (bread dough) 212–14

knocking back (bread dough) 16, 215–16

kumara & pumpkin salad with pear maple syrup & yoghurt 142

labne: middle eastern platter 66–68

laksa paste 237

lamb: beetroot, grilled lamb & haloumi salad 144
  lamb kofta 66
  marinade for 235, 238
  slow-roasted leg of lamb with olives & whisky 122

lemon: lemon cream mille-feuille 166
  lemon curd 243
  lemon dressing 237
  lemon icing 192
  salami & rocket with lemon dressing 20

levain (sourdough starter) 221–23
  global baker baguette traditional 34–35
  pain au levain 26–29

love heart jam dodgers 205

luxury milo fruit & nut slice 194

mango: israeli couscous, mango & pomegranate salad 106

marinade: asian 235
  mediterranean 238
  north african 238

marinated chargrilled capsicums 99

marinated kalamata olives 68

marshmallows in a sesame seed brandy snap puddle 208

mascarpone, vanilla honey-infused 170

mayonnaise 237; see also aïoli

dill mayonnaise 14–15
mediterranean green bean salad 75
middle eastern platter 66–68
mille-feuille: lemon cream 166
mini belgian biscuits 207
mini wholewheat irish soda bread
    sandwiches with smoked salmon,
    onion marmalade & dill mayonnaise
    14–15
mixing (bread dough) 212–14
moulding (bread dough) 215, 216
muffins: dairy-free banana & walnut soya
    190
    spiced summer berry compote 188
mushrooms: roasted field mushrooms
    240
    snowpea, mushroom & pancetta
    risotto 118
mussels: classic steamed mussels 138
    italian fish stew 116

nahm jim dressing 238
nougatine spoon 164
nuts 232; see also almond, pecan,
    walnut
    fruit & nut loaf 39
    luxury milo fruit & nut slice 194
    ultimate muesli breakfast scone
    56–57

olaf's vollkorn loaf 50
olive: marinated kalamata olives 68
    slow-roasted leg of lamb with olives &
    whisky 122
    sun-dried tomato, black olive &
    anchovy dip 92
    tapenade, with sun-dried tomato &
    cashew 238
onion marmalade 14–15, 18, 239 (jam)
osso bucco (venison) 120
oysters three ways (italian, japanese,
    spanish) 86

pain au levain: poilâne miche-style pain
    au levain 26–29
pancetta: snowpea, mushroom &
    pancetta risotto 118
panko: chicken tenders with panko 96
passionfruit: tropical passionfruit &
    coconut chocolate truffles 204

pasta: chocolate & blue cheese tortellini
    on praline 162
    summer pasta salad 150
    spaghetti puttanesca 110
    tomato sauce for pasta 235
pastry, butter puff 224–26
    plum & fennel tarte tatin 160
    lemon cream mille-feuille 166
    processing tips 225–26
pastry, short: black sesame seed 227
    black sesame seed-crusted vegetarian
    quiche 200
pastry, sweet 224
    almond frangipane fruit tartlets 198
    luxury milo fruit & nut slice 194
peach: poached peaches with prosciutto
    & gorgonzola 90
pear: red cabbage with pear & balsamic
    124
pecan: cinnamon & pecan easter quick
    bread twist 56
    triple chocolate chunk & pecan
    cookies 182
pesto: pesto verde 48, 239
    sun-dried tomato pesto 48, 241
pide, turkish 48–49
pizza base 239
    tomato sauce for pizza or pasta 235
plum & fennel tarte tatin with ice cream,
    apple purée & white chocolate tuiles
    160
poached peaches with prosciutto &
    gorgonzola 90
poilâne miche-style pain au levain
    26–29
pomegranate: israeli couscous, mango &
    pomegranate salad 106
    roast turkey with pomegranate &
    vanilla sauce 132
    syrup 244
pork: marinade for 238
    vietnamese lemongrass roasted ribs
    137
pot stickers: prawn, chilli & vietnamese-
    mint pot stickers 94
potato: truffle-infused mash 124
poussin: roast poussin with juniper,
    orange & black pepper 128
praline: chocolate & blue cheese tortellini
    on praline with caramel sauce 162

crunchy praline 243
prawn: green prawn curry 140
    prawn, chilli & vietnamese-mint pot
    stickers 94
preserved tomatoes 240
proof (bread dough) 216, 217
prosciutto: poached peaches with
    prosciutto & gorgonzola 90
pumpkin: beetroot, pumpkin, feta &
    roasted garlic quick bread 52
    kumara & pumpkin salad 142
    stuffed baked pumpkin 113

quiche: black sesame seed-crusted
    vegetarian quiche 200
quinoa: stuffed baked pumpkin with
    quinoa & prunes 113

raspberry: coulis 170, 244
    raspberry & strawberry compote
    166
red cabbage with pear & balsamic 124
risotto: snowpea, mushroom & pancetta
    risotto 118
roast poussin with juniper, orange &
    black pepper 128
roast turkey with pomegranate & vanilla
    sauce 132
rocket 20, 23
rolls, sunflower & paprika 16
root vegetable salad platter 146
rosé jelly with summer berries 158
rustico bread: fresh chunky apple,
    hazelnut, thyme & cabernet sauvignon
    rustico bread 30–33
rye flour 229
    pain au levain 26, 220

salad: avocado, grapefruit 78
    beetroot, grilled lamb & haloumi 144
    insalata caprese 77
    israeli couscous, mango & pomegranate
    106
    kumara & pumpkin 142
    mediterranean green bean 75
    rocket 23
    root vegetable salad platter 146
    summer pasta 150
salami & rocket with lemon dressing &
    goat's cheese bruschetta topping 20

salmon: mini wholewheat irish soda bread sandwiches with smoked salmon 14–15
   salmon tartare 62
salt 230–31
   salt brine for barbecued chicken 108
sauce: basic tomato sauce 235
   caramel sauce 242
   hot as hell sauce 131
   pomegranate & vanilla sauce 132
   toffee sauce 244
   thai sweet chilli sauce 241
savoury garden vegetable & cheese twist 46–47
scone dough 46
   ultimate muesli breakfast scone 56–57
seeding (bread) 217–18
sesame seed: black sesame seed-crusted vegetarian quiche 200
   black sesame seed short pastry 227
   marshmallows in a sesame seed brandy snap puddle 208
shortbread, cranberry 180
slow-roasted leg of lamb with olives & whisky 122
smoked fish, green bean & potato salad with horseradish dressing 134
snowpea, mushroom & pancetta risotto 118
soup: chicken, bacon & corn soup 72
   chilled avocado, lime & cucumber soup 80
   winter vegetable soup 82
sour cherry & cranberry trifle 155–57
sourdough 221–22; see also levain
   fig & aniseed sourdough loaf 36–39
   poilâne miche-style pain au levain 26–29
   starter 221–23
soya flour 230
   dairy-free banana & walnut soya muffin 190
spaghetti puttanesca 110
spiced summer berry compote muffins 188
spicy peanut dressing 149
spinach: goat's cheese, spinach & parsley dip 92
squid: italian blanched squid 71

sticky stem-ginger cake with lemon icing & ginger-syrup infused greek yoghurt 192
stollen: dresdner christmas stollen 43–45
strawberry: & cream truffles 206
   & raspberry compote 166
stuffed baked pumpkin with quinoa & prunes 113
sugar syrup 244
summer pasta salad 150
sun-dried tomato, black olive & anchovy dip 92
sunflower & paprika rolls served with antipasti 16
sunken chocolate cake with vanilla honey-infused mascarpone & raspberry coulis 170

tapas 20, 66; see also antipasti
tapenade: olive, sun-dried tomato & cashew 238
tart: almond frangipane fruit tartlets 198
   almond & walnut tartlets 168
   berry stella healthy tart 196
   plum & fennel tarte tatin 160
thai curry paste 240
thai sweet chilli sauce 241
tomato: gazpacho dressing 78
   insalata caprese 75
   olive, sundried tomato & cashew tapenade 238
   preserved tomatoes 240
   slow-roasted tomatoes 241
   sun-dried tomato pesto 241
   tomato & basil bruschetta topping 20
   tomato sauce for pasta or pizza 235
   sun-dried tomato, black olive & anchovy dip 92
tortellini: chocolate & blue cheese tortellini 162
traditional potted cheese 100
triple chocolate chunk & pecan cookies 182
tropical passionfruit & coconut chocolate truffles 204
truffle-infused mash 124
truffles
   tropical passionfruit & coconut chocolate truffles 204

strawberries & cream truffles 206
tuiles: orange 243–44
   white chocolate 161
turkey: roast turkey with pomegranate & vanilla sauce 132

udon noodles with seasonal vegetables & spicy peanut dressing 149
ultimate hot cross buns 41–42
ultimate muesli breakfast scone 56–57

vanilla: ice cream 245
   & pomegranate sauce 132
vegetable: black sesame seed-crusted vegetarian quiche 200
   root vegetable salad platter 146
   savoury garden vegetable & cheese twist 46–47
   udon noodles with seasonal vegetables 149
   winter vegetable soup 82
venison: osso bucco 121
vietnamese lemongrass roasted ribs 137
vinaigrette: double soy 236
   tarragon sherry 236

walnut: almond & walnut tartlets 168
   dairy-free banana & walnut soya muffin 190
wasabi & vietnamese mint dressing 241
wheat 228–30
wheat-free baking powder 241
whipped brie de meaux & crouton mille-feuille with rocket salad 25
white chocolate chunk & cranberry chewy cookies 176
wholemeal flour 229; see also wheat
   global baker baguette traditional 34–35
wholewheat bread 221
winter vegetable soup with israeli couscous & borlotti beans 82

yeast 234
yoghurt: ginger-syrup infused greek yoghurt 192
   labne 66

Dean Brettschneider is a professional baker and patissier. After completing his apprenticeship in New Zealand he worked in the US, Britain, Europe and the Middle East, gaining experience in all areas of the baking and patisserie world. Today, Dean is regarded as one of the best bakers on the planet. Following some years based in Shanghai, Dean is now working from Denmark and Britain, but still visits New Zealand regularly throughout each year and has bakery interests in Auckland and Shanghai. Dean's previous baking books have won World Food Media Awards and Gourmand World Cookbook Awards. Dean also appears as judge of the successful television series *Nestlé New Zealand's Hottest Home Baker* and in many other television programmes that promote baking excellence.

www.globalbaker.com

Mark McDonough owns Zarbo, one of the first big delicatessans in Auckland to offer a large range of local and imported food products and fresh café meals. Zarbo won Café of the Year in Michael Guy's Café magazine in 2008. Mark started in the hospitality industry as a university student, as a way of paying the bills, but then found it was more fun than studying. Although he has never trained formally as a chef, Mark has the main prerequisite: a deep-seated love of food and an understanding of flavour combinations. Mark lives in Auckland with his wife, Cushla, and two children, Felix and Olive. Mark's previous books have all been top sellers and reprinted several times.

www.zarbo.co.nz

Aaron McLean is an Auckland-based food, travel and lifestyle photographer. He works for many of New Zealand's leading magazines and his work has appeared in 15 books. His images have won *Cuisine* magazine MPA awards in the Home and Food category and the Supreme Award for best use of photography. In the 2009 Travcom Travel Media Awards, Aaron was the winner of the Best Series of Travel Images. In 2010 he was awarded a Golden Ladle at Le Cordon Bleu World Food Media Awards as Best Food Photographer.

www.aaronmclean.com